Scor
2025

(Annual, Monthly, Daily Horoscope 2025)

Dr Gautam DK
Naresh Gautam

First Edition Sep 2024

Prayer

|| om gaṁ gaṇapataye namaḥ ||

|| brahmā murāristripurāntakārī bhānuḥ śaśī bhūmisuto budhaśca guruśca

śukraḥ śanirāhuketavaḥ sarve grahāḥ śānti karā bhavantu ||

Brahmā (the Creator), Murāri (Vishnu, the Sustainer), Tripurāntakarin (Siva, the slayer of the demon Tripurāsura), Bhānu (the Sun), Shashin (the Moon), Bhūmisuta (Mars, the son of the Earth), Budha (Mercury), Guru (Jupiter), Shukra (Venus), Shani (Saturn), Rāhu and Ketu, may all these Grahas be peaceful.

Books by the Author

General Series

1. Marriage Astrology
2. Matchmaking for Marriage
3. Love Marriage
4. Mangal Dosha
5. Lal Kitab
6. Astrology for Beginners- Twelve Houses of Chart Vol I
7. Astrology for Beginners – Planets in Astrology Vol II
8. Astrology for Beginners – 12 Zodiac Signs Vol III
9. Ashwini Nakshatra
10. Bharani Nakshatra
11. World of Souls
12. Vastu Made Simple

Planet Series

13. Rahu Nature and Behaviour
14. Rahu in Twelve Houses of Chart
15. Rahu in Twelve Houses of Chart (Hindi)
16. Ketu in Twelve Houses of Chart
17. Mercury in Astrology
18. Jupiter in Twelve Houses of Chart
19. Saturn in Twelve Houses of Chart

Annual Horoscope 2024

20- 29 (Aries, Gemini, Cancer, Leo, Virgo, Libra, Sagittarius, Capricorn, Aquarius, Pisces)

30. Rahu Ketu Transit 2023-25

Annual Horoscope 2025

31. Aries Horoscope 2025
32. Taurus Horoscope 2025

Table of Contents

INTRODUCTION

As we bid farewell to 2024 and greet the New Year 2025, we embrace the hope that comes with new beginnings. Time is in constant flux, and the future remains a mystery, offering both trials and opportunities.

Let's explore what your Zodiac Sign stores for you in 2025. What lies ahead for you regarding education, love, marriage, children, career, promotions, business expansion, financial prospects, debt clearance, health, property, travels, social networks, and new ventures?

I want to cover this annual horoscope in seven chapters. In the first chapter, we will cover the transit of planets in the year 2025 and its implications at a mundane level and how the movement of planets is going to affect the world on various fronts geopolitics, politics, economy, finances, food production, tourism and healthcare. In the second chapter, we will cover the important dates during which major events at the mundane level will happen. These two chapters will be common for the Annual Horoscope 2025 series.

In the third chapter, we will cover the Year 2025 for that zodiac sign, which is based on the transit of major planets and conjunctions affecting for a longer duration. Here we will be covering the Year 2025 predictions in terms of general, profession, finances, health, love life and marriage, progeny, education, and spiritualism

In the fourth chapter, we will go through month-wise predictions for the zodiac sign. These predictions will be primarily based upon the transit of the Sun and then the effect of other planets. This will be precise to plan the activity for each month.

In the fifth chapter, we go through the particular dates of each month in the year 2025 and their likely effect on the zodiac sign. This will cover the results at the two-day level as it will be based on the movement of the Moon in various signs. In the second part of this chapter, we will be covering the daily predictions. This will be based on the transit of the Moon over various Nakshatras. This will help to plan the day-to-day activity for the entire year.

In the sixth chapter, we will cover the basic characteristics of your zodiac sign. In the seventh chapter, we will cover a few remedies that should be carried out by this Zodiac sign native.

From Aries to Pisces, each sign will experience different opportunities and challenges, tailored to their personality traits. The positions of planets indeed influence events in a person's life in their birth chart. The timing of these events is determined by the planetary periods and the planetary transits indicate when the results of those events will manifest. **If an event is not promised in the birth chart and is not aligned with the current planetary periods, the transits might not significantly impact.**

The concept of Desh (place), Kaal (time), and Patar (individual) plays a crucial role in shaping the outcomes of astrological influences. Results vary based on geographical location, time, and the individual's unique circumstances.

Destiny is a complex interplay of cosmic influences, personal choices, and life circumstances. It's a dynamic interaction that can guide, but not completely dictate, the course of one's life. While the stars influence us, remember, it's our own choices (free will) that shape our destiny. Keep in mind that the future isn't fixed, and our decisions create our reality.

As a disclaimer, I would like to mention that the future is unpredictable and no one in the world can give assurance that an event will happen and with what intensity. We, astrologers, try to decipher with the best of our capabilities and intentions so that we can guide mankind to prepare themselves for any eventuality.

Let's welcome the transformative energies of 2025 and make it a year of growth, joy, and self-discovery. May this book be your guiding light, leading you to your dreams. We wish you a year filled with cosmic blessings and endless possibilities!

****

2025: ASTROLOGICAL OVERVIEW

Based on the position and movement of planets in 2025, we need to decipher how this will affect the world on various fronts, such as the world economy, politics, finances, food production, tourism, and healthcare.

The planetary position as of 01 Jan 2025 at 00.01 hrs will be as under:

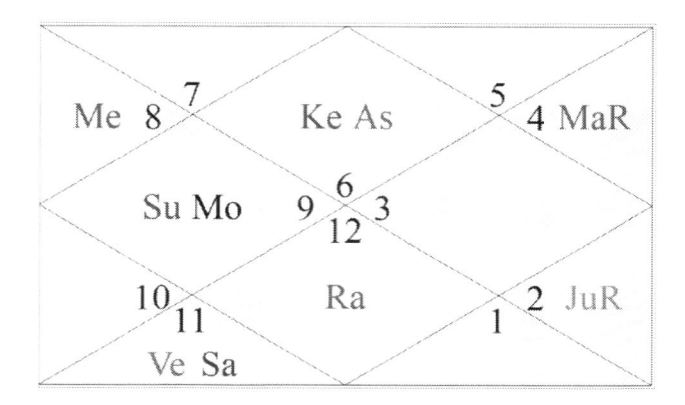

We will go through the transit of planets in the period 01 Jan to 31 Dec 2025 and try to decipher their implications. We consider the Kaal Purush Kundli (natural horoscope) for world events.

Jupiter in transit in the Taurus sign, has been retrograde since 09 Oct 2024 and will be direct on 4 Feb 2025. Jupiter enters Gemini on 14 May 2025 and Cancer on 18 Oct 2025. Jupiter becomes retrograde for 119 days and on 11 Nov 2025 and re-enters Gemini sign on 05 Dec

2025. Apart from this, it will remain combust from 22 June to 16 July 2025. During the combustion period, there are no auspicious activities or functions planned.

Saturn is in transit in the Aquarius sign in the year 2023. It will transit to Pisces sign on 29 Mar 2025. Saturn goes for retrogradation from 13 July to 28 Nov 2025 for 139 days. With Saturn transit in Aquarius since 2023, Sade Sati is going on for Pisces, Aquarius and Capricorn signs. These three signs are facing a lot of problems and obstacles in their life due to Saturn's Sade Sati effect. Saturn will transit to Pisces on 29 Mar 2025 and with this, the Sade Sati of Capricorn will be over but Sade Sati for Aries will begin.

During this period, Mars which is retrograde in Cancer since 07 Dec 2024 will re-enter in Gemini sign on 21 Jan 2025. Mars becomes direct on 24 Feb 2025 and transit to Cancer on 3 Apr 2025, Leo on 7 June 2025, Virgo on 28 Jul 2025, Scorpio on 27 Oct 2025, and Sagittarius on 7 Dec 2025.

Details of Venus and Mercury's transit are given at the end of the book. Venus will be retrograde from 2 Mar to 13 Apr 2025. Mercury will be retrograde from 15 Mar to 07 Apr 2025 in Pisces, 18 July to 11 Aug 2025 in Cancer, 10 Nov to 29 Nov 2025 in Scorpio/ Libra.

Mercury generally retrogrades for a period of 20 to 24 days. During the retrogradation of Mercury, there may be a reversal in actions and speech, indicating shifts in speech abilities, communication skills, and decision-making abilities. People will tend to display either highly introverted or highly extroverted behavior. They may tend to express themselves excessively or may struggle to express themselves at all. At times, they can make unpredictable or sudden decisions that surprise others. Period 15 Mar to 07 Apr 2025, when Mercury conjuncts with Rahu and later on 18 Mar 2025, Saturn Joins, the period will be quite challenging as the decisions made during this period may be disastrous.

In the year 2025, there will be two lunar (13-14 Mar 2025 and 07-08 Sep 2025) and two solar (29 Mar 2025 and 21 Sep 2025) eclipses. Details are given at the end of the book. These eclipses assume importance and can cause various unpleasant events in the world. You may observe incidents within 20-30 days of their occurrence.

Geopolitics

Countries and political parties will make new alliances. You will find major shifts in existing alliances as enemies of one time may become friends. I find India's relations with Western countries further improving. Even after 14 May 2025, once Jupiter moves to Gemini, India continue to grow as a more responsible and powerful country. Other countries may look to India for guidance and help and India emerge as stronger. India will be treated as Vishwaguru, or a guide or someone who can resolve conflicts between the countries. India may initiate talks with Pakistan or will provide some relief during its crisis. India may become a guiding factor for other countries. India will stand with every country which faces a major crisis.

You may notice that during this period, the religious conversion issue will be in focus. Till 18 May 2025, Rahu in Jupiter house is indicative of large-scale conversions to the religious belief system. This may be by force luring them with money or indoctrination by their religious leaders. fundamentalists will try to hijack the agenda and dominate the government and the public. Demand for a separate homeland or to implement laws based on religion will increase causing protests in several countries. Religious fundamentalism will rise further and start disturbing the law and order of many countries.

After 18 May 2025, few countries or religious lobbies may ally to counter the religious fundamentalist forces. There may be a further rise of ISIS or any new organisation or some Christians may rise against Muslim fundamentalism. Few countries may look seriously at the refugee issue and may take some strong action. Governments will try to control the religious conversion momentum.

During the period Mar 2025 to July 2025, one solar and one lunar eclipse are being observed apart from Kaal Sarp Yoga. It creates a war-like situation between different countries. War may or may not happen but weapon industry lobbies will try to create a situation when countries will increase purchases of weapons and material of destruction.

In my annual horoscope for 2024, I have already predicted that the situation may aggravate further resulting in the involvement of more countries in this war. The war is going to be between two different religious ideologies which may have devastating effects. Collateral damage in Ghaza is likely to create a new breeding ground for terrorism and feed terrorist organisations like Hamas. Muslim population worldwide is going to create a wave of sympathisers and more countries will get entangled in this. Struggle between Muslim and non-Muslim populations may create a major rift. If the issues are not resolved then you will find a greater number of countries will get involved in this creating a situation of world War and the most probable period is when Rahu and Saturn conjunct in Mar to May 2025.

The collateral damages in Ghaza have given a forum to various groups all over the US, UK and EU countries where they are putting pressure on Govt to cut ties with Israel. Initially, govt ignored those protests but now governments are using force to control those protests. The settlement of Palestine refugees also become a major issue. Iran also fired at Israel and the UN is trying to put pressure on Israel to stop the war. Though Israel will be completing its offensive in Ghaza, liberation of Ghaza from Israel will be an issue of discord which will become a reason for instability in the entire region. There is the possibility of more and more countries getting involved in this turmoil. The situation will be critical during the period Mar to May 2025.

European Union will pass through a difficult phase of staying together as there will be a lot of discontentment and disagreement. The war between Ukraine and Russia may become nonrelevant as Ukraine finally agrees not to join NATO.

India's relationship with the US may be stressed as both countries for their national interests and under pressure from the media may have conflict issues.

Politics

Saturn's position in Aquarius, its Mool-trikona Sign, holds great significance, particularly in areas related to career, government, politics, and foreign affairs. Once Saturn transits to Pisces, which is the sign of Jupiter, there may be ups and downs in the political arena. Political parties will develop new strategies and try to destabilize existing elected governments worldwide. Misuse of deep fake videos using AI for propaganda will emerge as another battleground. Foreign countries will try to destabilize Indian democracy. The South China Sea may become active and reason for confrontation between the countries.

Economy

Stock markets will continue to grow in the year 2025, as Jupiter is progressing towards the Cancer sign, which is a sign of its exaltation.

There will be a surge in economic activities. All sectors will boom and give good results. Jupiter gets exalted in the Cancer sign and as it moves towards its exaltation sign, the financial sector booms. Stock markets and Gold will give good results.

Correction in the stock market will be observed after 11 Nov 2025, when Jupiter becomes retrograde. This correction may be for the duration of five to six months. Then markets will again rebound to new levels. This upward trend may continue till Dec 2026. Thereafter I find the markets will be looking for a correction. Prices of Gold and even property may also rise during the same time frame and thereafter look for correction. That correction may not be instant but at a gradual pace.

The year 2025 will provide much relief to everyone. The economic sector will grow, providing more and more employment opportunities of job. However, the Jobs will be skilled or knowledge-based industry rather than semiskilled. Artificial intelligence will continue to replace the human workforce. Those who upgrade themselves will be able to survive otherwise will perish. The world will continue to depend on unskilled labour, but the demand for the same will continue to fall.

The property market will escalate after May 2025, as Saturn will transit in Pisces and this trend will continue for the next 2.5 years. There may be some correction during the retrograde periods of Jupiter and Saturn.

Technology

There may be technological advancement in the internet or communication. 6G technology will be launched and brought into use. Space technology may get a boost. AI usage will increase and threaten the semi-skilled industry. Due to the Saturn Pisces connection, some new viruses may emerge, and antivirus for the same will be developed. In the meantime, there may be a loss of lives.

Tourism

Rahu in the Aquarius sign after 18 May 2025, is quite indicative of increased trends in travels to foreign countries. The trend to visit foreign countries will increase. The business of travel agents and tour operators will outgrow. The travel agencies and tour operators will make a lot of money. However, the public will be looking for countries having cheaper cost of living.

Food Production

Rahu transit in Pisces till 18 May 2025, the exaltation sign of Venus indicates an increase in means to enjoyment. Life standards of people will improve as more consumer products will penetrate the markets. On 29 Mar 2025, Saturn will transit to Pisces and aspect Taurus, sign of Venus. Taurus is a sign of the entertainment and food industry. Jupiter presence in Taurus from 01 May 2024 to 14 May 2025 indicates that the entertainment and hospitality business will boom. They may adopt new means to reach the masses, especially after the Artificial intelligence and chat GPT. New platforms will emerge to replace the old systems. All the creator needs to upgrade themselves to meet the technology challenges. This advice applies to all people involved in the entertainment industry and hospitality business.

In 2025, there will be bumper production of food grains as Jupiter will expand the reservoirs of food grains. Technology such as the usage of Drones and genetically modified seeds will enhance food production. The commodity market will get a boost. However, the production of crops after May 2025 will drop. There may be famine or critical food shortage in a few countries. But the world has become one at the commodity level so famine in one place does not mean much scarcity of food, provided you have money.

Healthcare

Healthcare systems may witness a crash during the period Mar to July 2025 as new bacteria or viruses affecting the digestive system may come up. This disease will affect the stomach and digestion-related issues. A lot of people in healthcare will be infected due to this disease. One of the reasons for the spread of the same may be contaminated and infected water or air. The healthcare industry will make a fortune out of this disease. The situation will affect a large population in the world.

Disasters

After 29 Mar 2025, Saturn will transit to Pisces the last zodiac sign, indicating detachment, transformation, expenditure and losses. During Saturn transit in the water sign, you may find cases or increases in hurricanes, cyclones, earthquakes, oil spills, pollution of water, nuclear leakages, pollution of water bodies, deficient rainfall, etc.

Events During the Periods

12 Feb to 14 Apr 2025

Sun conjunct with Saturn in Aquarius sign from 12 Feb to 14 Mar 2025. Sun is in transit over Saturn indicating the state of disagreement between the public and government. There may be a lot of unrest, agitations and law and order problems. Death of any senior renowned politician can happen during this time. The government may try to implement some orders which are not acceptable to a few sections of society. Resulting unrest.

Rahu Sun conjunct in Pisces sign from 14 Mar to 14 Apr 2025. Saturn joins the conjunction on 29 Mar 2025. Rahu can corrupt the government authorities and they can use their powers arbitrarily without any justifications. Sun Rahu or Mars Rahu conjunction indicates fires, accidents or heat waves. In March – April 2025, again some major tragedy will take place which may be related to water and heat. Terrorist activities or riot-like situations cannot be overruled during this period.

Major Alert: 29 Mar to 29 July 2025

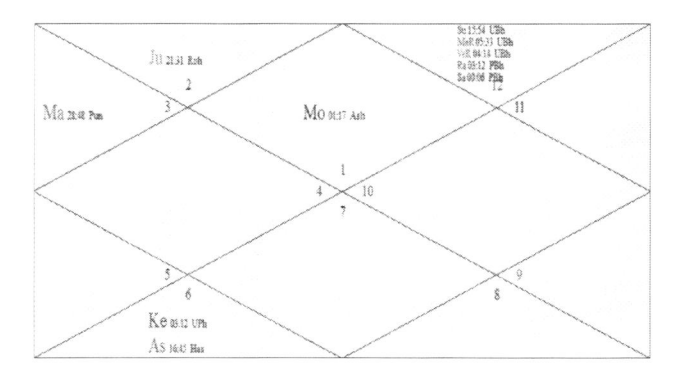

Saturn transit in Pisces on 29 Mar 2025 and conjunct with Rahu till 18 May 2025. This period may be one of the worst, as, during April 2025, Sun, Mercury and Venus will be under the effect of Rahu and Saturn. Mars will be in debilitation and that indicates a major problem at the Mundane level. During this period, there may be a major loss of lives, property and human rights due to war between countries, diseases or terrorist action. You may notice that Kaal Sarp Yoga is being formed from 29 Mar 2025 to 29 July 2025. This may be the time when terrorist organisations attack Western countries. Presently, Israel is in the process of finishing the Hamas, a terrorist wing of Palestine. In the process and excessive use of force, there will be a lot of collateral damage. Remember collateral damage creates more enmity and the resultant force emerging is more lethal, evolved and dangerous. Those forces may try to cause a lot of instability worldwide.

If we go down history, the similar planetary position of Kaal Sarp Yoga was formed from June to Sep 2005. Several unpleasant events happened during that period. On 07 July 2005, four coordinated suicide bombings hit central London, killing 52 people and injuring over 700. On 23 July 2005, a series of bombings hit the resort city of Sharm el-Sheikh, Egypt, killing over 80 people. On 14 Aug, a flight crashed in Greece killing 121 passengers and crew. On 16 Aug 2005, another flight crashed in Venezuela, killing 160 passengers and crew. On 29 Aug 2005, Hurricane Katrina made landfall along the U.S. Gulf Coast, causing severe damage, killing over a thousand people and dealing an estimated Billions of Dollars damage. On 31 Aug 2005, a stampede at the Al-Aaimmah bridge in Baghdad, Iraq, killed 953. On 08 Oct 2005, a 7.6 Mw Kashmir earthquake struck Pak Occupied Kashmir, killing more than 86,000 people and displacing several million more.

This time, the planet's position will be worse when Rahu and Saturn conjunct in the Pisces sign, and Kaal Sarp Yoga is formed. At the mundane level, there may be several calamities, accidents, and disasters. However, life continues as nature destroys to keep a balance in the ecosystem.

15 May to 16 Jul 2025

Jupiter's Sun conjunction in Taurus / Gemini, from 15 May to 16 July 2025, will bring positive results for financial sectors. This will be a time for the Banking sector to grow, and accordingly, stock prices of Banks may notice a spike. This is a time of positivity for the Public. There will be an increase in financial status. Industries will grow with the support of the government. Remember that before this period, there will be a major correction in the market.

07 June to 28 July 2025

Mars Ketu conjunction from 07 June to 28 July 2025 is being formed in Leo sign, fiery sign. Ketu and Mars energies may result in fire, terrorist attacks, and natural disasters in mountainous terrain in a few countries. Leo is a fire sign and Mars is a fiery planet with Ketu, a planet of destruction that will affect nature, forests and land. There may be landslides, and settlement of ground resulting in damage to buildings. Sun and Mars both represent energy. This period also coincides with the summer season when you find fire incidents in several places. This period may also witness air accidents, train accidents, industrial accidents, or major fire incidents.

17 Aug to 15 Sep 2025

Sun and Ketu conjunction is being formed in the Leo sign from 17 Aug to 16 Sep 2025 may bring turbulence for ruling governments. In some states, there may be trading of elected candidates to form various alliances, destabilize the ruling party and form their government. All over the world, you may notice that opposition parties may try to destabilize the ruling government by ethical or unethical means. Terrorist activities will emerge in a new form and higher intensity. Sun is eclipsed by Ketu and indicates trouble in law and order, the death of a popular world leader and an increase in terrorist activities. To control the law-and-order situation, governments have to take some strong steps which can cause mass unrest.

Leo is related to the stomach and digestive system. Diseases related to the stomach may surface as epidemics during this period.

16 Nov 2025 to 14 Jan 2026

Sun-Mars conjunction is being formed in Scorpio and later Sagittarius sign. Sun and Mars energies indicate that the authorities become tyrants and make decisions that may not be democratic or for the welfare of the public. They force their ways to achieve their targets. This period may witness some major clashes between govt and various rebel groups. This may turn out to be violent in Nov 2025. It can have some connection with new laws which will be passed by governments in various countries. Those laws may be against religious conversion or migration-related. Like Europe or Western countries such as the US, the UK may impose certain restrictions on the migration of refugees, population control, etc which may give rise to anti-government campaigns. In India, these could be related to the construction of the temple at the site which has been converted to a mosque after the demolition of the temple. Kashi Vishwanath or Mathura temple may come into focus during this period. Govt may take action on certain parties based on their involvement in corruption or anti-national activities.

These are expected events in 2025, which are being predicted based on the transit or conjunction of major planets. The exact location and gravity of incidents cannot be ascertained due to our limited knowledge.

In the next chapters, I have endeavored to provide predictions for each zodiac sign, which should be considered with both your Moon Sign and Lagna. You can explore how this upcoming transit might introduce new opportunities or challenges in your life and the lives of your family members.

SCORPIO HOROSCOPE 2025

The year 2025, is going to give mixed results as all the major planets, Jupiter, Rahu, Ketu and Saturn will change their signs in the year 2025. During the first part of the year 2025, Scorpio is going to be blessed with good fortune, a happy married life, improvement in professional life and social relations. However, as the year progresses, there will be some challenges in health and married life.

Coming to the Horoscope 2025 for Scorpio sign, the astrological chart as of 01 Jan 2025 for Scorpio will be as under: -

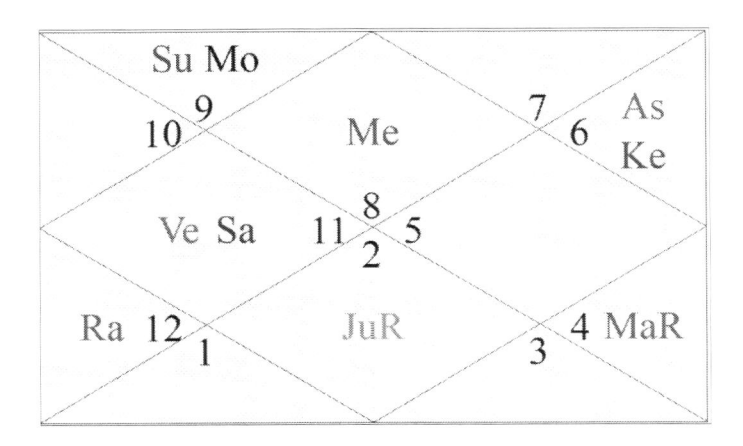

During the first part of the year 2025, the Scorpio is having a lot of positivity due to Jupiter in the seventh house.

Until 29 Mar 2025, Saturn will be transiting through your fourth house, a phase known as Kantaka Sani. Over the past two and a half years, you may have experienced increased family responsibilities, which could have brought stress or a heightened sense of duty. Unresolved emotional issues might resurface during this period, pushing you to confront and heal them. Concerns about your health or your mother's health could arise, and there may be difficulties, including probable harassment from authorities. Financial challenges could occur, as savings may be drained by unnecessary or wasteful expenses. You may also be compelled to relocate or move away from your home. You need to be cautious while driving as vehicular accidents may happen. You may suffer and have some losses during travel. Despite any struggle or obstacles, the outcome will be positive.

On a positive note, this period can foster personal growth, helping you better understand and manage your emotions. You might focus on creating a more stable and secure home environment, possibly through renovations, moving, or cultivating a more supportive family dynamic. Long-term investments in property or family matters may become a consideration.

After 29 Mar 2025, Saturn lord of the third and fourth house transit to the fifth house. Saturn in the fifth house will bring positive vibes in the matter of children, love relationships and creative pursuits. Nothing comes easy when Saturn is watching so work harder to have some positivity. Students have to work harder to achieve success. During the Saturn transit in the fifth house, till 3 June 2027, you may have to mourn the loss of some near relative or friend. Certain health issues and some pains regarding the legs may re-emerge. Your enemies will gain strength and try to create problems on all fronts.

The period between 29 Mar to 18 May 2025, when Rahu and Saturn conjunct in the fifth house, will create a lot of struggle and confusion in relationships, children and education matters. Your saved money may be spent on wasteful and unnecessary expenses, leading to financial difficulties.

Until 14 May 2025, Jupiter is in transit through your seventh house, bringing you pleasure, money, and other benefits through your spouse or partnership. You will get respite from all the major problems. Your financial status will improve, and you might receive awards and rewards from the government. You may acquire items of luxuries which may even be high-class vehicles. If you are unmarried, you might marry someone wealthy or from a good family background. This will lead to progress in your life, and you will succeed in your education. Money will come to you from various sources and savings will increase. You will find that your spouse, who may not have been cooperative before, will now become an ideal partner, providing you with all the pleasures and support you need. You will work towards a noble goal and succeed in it. You might travel to religious places and undertake business trips abroad, gaining benefits from them. If you are planning for a Child, you may be blessed with a child now. Due to your nature and behavior people will be attracted towards you and you will become a scholar admired by many.

After 14 May 2025, Jupiter lord of the second and fifth houses in the eighth house is likely to bring challenges in career, finances, education, love relationships, married life and progeny. For females, Jupiter is the significator of married life and life partner and its being in the eighth house, indicates some challenges for married life or the health of the life partner. There may be a loss of trust or disagreement over some trivial issues. You may find that the higher authorities are against you. The professional appreciation or recognition that you are expecting is being delayed due to conspiracy or unknown reasons. There might be some challenges that you have to encounter after the middle of the year in your career, however, there is nothing to be worried about. These hurdles will remain for a temporary period. You must keep control of your negative thoughts. This period will be conducive to spiritual activities, and you may consider planning visits to religious places. With the influence of Jupiter in the eighth and Ketu in the tenth house, Scorpio people will find themselves drawn towards a more spiritual path and less to their professional needs.

On 18 Oct 2025, Jupiter will transit to the ninth house, in the Cancer sign. Jupiter in this house will bring positivity to life. The period till 11 Nov 2025 will be quite positive and bring favorable results in luck, finances, education, progeny and family affairs. This can be time for auspicious outcomes such as increased wealth, career success, and happiness in personal life. Jupiter's influence will also encourage creative ideas and involvement in charitable, spiritual, or religious activities. You will feel pride in your children's growth and development, and your creative potential will be enhanced. Financial gains are likely, and your love life will expand. The period remains quite positive for your education, love matters, progeny and your creative pursuits.

Until 18 May 2025, the nodal planets Rahu and Ketu will be transiting through Pisces and Virgo, affecting your fifth and eleventh houses, respectively. With Jupiter's influence from the seventh house, you can expect a steady income from multiple sources, and you'll enjoy material comforts. Career growth is on the horizon, with your hard work paying off, but success will require effort and persistence. You may excel in politics, gaining popularity and climbing the ladder of success. However, the Rahu-Ketu axis in your love and social life may bring challenges. In your love life, conflicts and misunderstandings could arise, leading to turbulence in your relationship. Friendships may also face strain, with issues causing ongoing stress. While some friends will remain loyal, problems in social circles might lead to a tarnished reputation, possibly due to involvement in questionable activities.

After 18 May 2025, the nodal planets Rahu and Ketu will be in transit to Aquarius and Leo signs, fourth and tenth house respectively. Rahu can create disputes with the mother, relatives, and family due to property. Rahu here also affects the native's happiness and comforts and lack of maternal love or support from others. Healthwise, Rahu in this house indicates an emotional imbalance, fear of the unknown, mental disturbances and heart issues. You may be traveling abroad or long distances from home due to job requirements. There will be a period of separation from the mother or the health of the mother may be an issue of concern.

Due to Ketu's transit in the tenth house, you may be drawn towards a more spiritual path and feel detached from professional emotions or responsibilities. Though the job may be secured you may not like to put in your best efforts. You may also show little interest in social status and would like to adopt a non-traditional approach in your career which may even be changing the career. You may experience fluctuating career paths, unconventional occupations, frequent shifts in your chosen field, unexpected shifts or disruptions in your professional path. On the positive side, you will be quite confident with your professional knowledge and may be promoted or upgraded. Few Scorpios may find that their professional status has been enhanced with more responsibility.

Once Saturn goes retrograde from 13 July to 28 Nov 2025 and Jupiter retrograde from 11 Nov 2025 to 11 Mar 2026, you will find certain unpredictable events happening in life.

Overall, the year 2025, is going to bring some challenges in the subjects of health and relationships, however, there is nothing to be worried about. These hurdles will remain for a temporary period. You must keep control of your negative thoughts and your temper, or you might end up losing some favorable connections with your friends and family. You are going to experience a rich period of personal growth and a flourishing career if you follow the right path and work hard.

Considering the general effects of the transit of planets, let us go through the effects of the transit of planets concerning the profession, finances, health, love life and marriage, progeny, education and spiritualism.

Career

Saturn is the natural significator of the profession, while in a Scorpio chart, the Sun, as the lord of the tenth house, also represents career matters. Jupiter, being a naturally benefic planet, is associated with finances, well-being, and career. Therefore, in a Scorpio chart, the Sun, Jupiter, and Saturn are the key planets influencing one's profession. Their strength and placement in the natal chart play a crucial role in determining career growth and success.

Your career and business are off to a positive start this year, thanks to Jupiter's transit in the seventh house in the first part of the year. Saturn initially in the fourth and later in the fifth house is likely to give overall good results.

Until 14 May 2025, Jupiter transit in the seventh house in Taurus, you can expect a period of positive developments in your career. The seventh house is associated with business, partnership and your image in society. The period holds promising prospects for launching your brand in a different company. Your new business idea is set to progress, and launching your venture will prove fruitful, leading to significant profits. Embrace this success to seek even better opportunities. The financial gains from a new venture may not be as promising as expected as the start of any new venture is connected to higher expenditures and fewer gains. You will be blessed with rewards, including wealth, fame, prosperity, and a prominent name. You will be highly motivated to create a positive and lasting impression in the public eye. However, if you are not recognized or appreciated, you may feel disheartened and become angry. There may be professional improvements and support from unexpected sources. You may become head of the organization. You will find success, financial gains and enhancement of your position. You will get additional responsibilities. Sometimes gains may not be in terms of money but can be in terms of popularity or other additional advantages linked to our position.

After 14 May 2025, Jupiter transits to the eighth house, and on 18 May 2025, Ketu transits into the tenth house, which is the house of profession. The tenth house is associated with career, public image, reputation, achievements, and the individual's role in society. Ketu being in the tenth house, the house of a profession gives you the energy to undergo any work pressure. You will be confident in your professional domain and not satisfied with the management. You would like to change the job or are forced to leave the job. You may get a job with higher responsibilities and better status but dissatisfaction and changes are quite possible. You may find a sense of disconnection or dissatisfaction in your career. You may find it difficult to establish a clear career path or may frequently change jobs. You may feel detached from the professional responsibilities and may divert towards spiritual or unconventional careers, such as those in healing, astrology, or other mystical practices. Jupiter in the eighth house from 14 May to 18 Oct 2025 further promotes that idea. You could give priority to spiritual or personal fulfillment over material success which could further create challenges in maintaining professional image and cause conflicts with bosses or figures of authority.

Due to Jupiter's transit in the eighth house, certain medical issues may divert you from professional responsibilities, which need to be addressed.

Saturn transit in the fifth house after 29 Mar 2025, indicates that you may be having struggles and obstacles in professional life. During the year 2025, if your job is not permanent as a government job, then the chances of job changes are very high. Even those who are in permanent jobs may dislocate for r professional reasons or they may be under a lot of pressure. During Saturn's retrograde motion from 13 Jul to 28 Nov 2025, you might face further hurdles, and gains achieved earlier could be reversed. Beware of potential conspiracies from colleagues during this time, as their support may wane. Any emotional decision-making during this period may have consequences so make professional choices with care and prudence.

Finances

In the Scorpio chart, Jupiter is the lord of the second house, the house of finances. Jupiter is the natural significator of finances. The position of Jupiter in the natal chart indicates the position of finances and savings.

Ketu being in the eleventh house until 18 May 2025, may create some sort of detachment from the materialistic world and you remain interested in spirituality and detachment. You need to be cautious about that and make deliberate decisions rather than being carried away by emotions.

Until 14 May 2025, Jupiter's position in the seventh house indicates that Jupiter will bless you with good finances. Income and savings both will be sufficient. You are likely spending these savings on investments like home renovations, property acquisition, purchasing a vehicle, or settling old debts.

After 14 May 2025, as Jupiter transits in the eighth house, you might encounter some financial challenges, so it's important to be cautious about your finances. Before making any risky decisions, carefully consider the potential outcomes, as there's a chance of losing money. While your income will be satisfactory, your expenses could also rise. To manage this, you'll need to control your spending to align with your earnings. While you may be tempted to make significant purchases, it's recommended to restrain your costly hobbies to prevent potential financial strain.

After 18 Oct 2025, once Jupiter transits to the ninth house, you will have multiple sources of income. Your finances and source of finances will get a boost from your family. You may gain financially from your foreign contacts, hospital and pharmaceutical industries, travel or hospitality business and even from legal matters. The period appears favorable for long-term investments in the stock market.

After 11 Nov 2025, as Jupiter becomes retrograde there may be some challenges and unexpected obstacles in the career. Do not rush to change jobs or fight with your senior as you may land in trouble at a professional level. That period is just to wait for the right opportunity and not to take any risks.

Love Life and Marriage

The period Until 14 May 2025 and then 18 Oct to 11 Nov 2025, holds the potential for significant changes in love matters and marriage. Jupiter's favorable position promises well for love relationships, marriage, and overall luck. For singles, this period brings promising opportunities for love. This is a promising time to potentially meet your soul mate, the person you've been seeking. If the timing aligns, marriage may be on the horizon, and it is advisable for those already in a relationship to consider getting married during this period. However, be rest assured that Saturn in the fifth house will create some resistance but finally, it will promise you a mature and devoted partner with strong bonds. Unmarried individuals may find a suitable match, making this a promising time to potentially meet your soulmate. Those in the process of finding a life partner may see their search come to fruition, and if the timing aligns with favorable Dasha periods, marriage could be a possibility.

There may be growth in your family or a significant family event where you'll play a major role, possibly as a sponsor. This could involve expenses for a family function. Those looking to have children may conceive during this period, and there will be happiness from your mother, family, and home. You will have the opportunity to travel with your family to distant and religious locations. Traveling with your partner to a dream destination may help rekindle the passion and excitement, leading to new beginnings and shared experiences. This could be a transformative journey for both of you, strengthening your bond and creating lasting memories.

During the period 14 May to 18 Oct 2025, Jupiter transits in the eighth house, which is considered the house of obstacles and obstructions, implying it may not be as beneficial for married life, especially for females. Jupiter's positioning in the eighth position could lead to challenges in married life for some individuals. For married people, they may find some suffocation in their love relations. That may be due to the reason that you have started having big plans and you find your love relations are not matching your expectations, so you trying to avoid meeting them. Take your time and don't rush into matters of love.

The period from 29 Mar to 18 May 2025 may be stressful for married life. There will be challenges in married life for some individuals. Saturn's aspect the Jupiter further creates challenges regarding health and married life.

The period from 15 Sep to 09 Oct 2025, when Ketu conjuncts with Venus in the Leo sign, is period of difficult time in relationship. You have to be careful regarding the health of your life partner or mutual relations.

<u>Education</u>

The period until 14 May and later from 18 Oct to 11 Nov 2025, is quite positive for students. Those who are looking to go abroad for higher education may find a positive period. There is an opportunity to get admission to the desired institute, go abroad or long distance for higher education. Those who are in the field of research or higher education will do well. Those who want to do an internship with foreign universities that can further translate to the job may find great opportunities. Saturn in the fifth house expects you to work hard and have patience. You may find some last-minute hitch, but if you continue in your efforts, you will be successful.

During the period 14 May to 18 Oct 2025, there may be some challenges and unexpected obstacles. One needs to put in his best and not try to find the shortcut or unethical means to get promoted in education. Jupiter is the planet of Dharma and ethics and do not expect a person should cheat.

The year 2025 holds the potential for achievements in your studies. It is important to stay focused on your studies and not get diverted. There may be some challenges and problems with learning and interests but finally, it turns out to be positive. Your efforts in exams are likely to bring positive results, and if you're studying engineering, concentrating on your project could be beneficial.

Progeny

The period until 14 May and later from 18 Oct to 11 Nov 2025, is quite positive for progeny. Scorpio can be blessed with a child in particular a Male child if his natal chart promises.

For the period 14 May to 18 Oct 2025, you must be very careful in progeny and you should go for regular medical check-ups.

Health

The start of the year 2025 will be quite positive in terms of health. Jupiter transit in the seventh house till 14 May 2025 and aspect lagna will bestow you with good health. Jupiter provides you protection from any chronic disease but minor health issues cannot be ruled out.

After 29 Mar 2025, Saturn's transit in the Pisces sign causes pains in feet and legs and leg injury generally below knee level. Those who have health issues related to digestion, diabetes or liver need to take regular medicine. Professional issues may keep you busy and divert you from your daily exercise routine which will affect your health.

Be attentive during the period 29 Mar to 18 May 2025. Energies of two malefic planets, Rahu and Saturn working in the fifth house may cause digestion-related issues.

After 18 May 2025, the Rahu and Ketu axis in the fourth and tenth will cause problems like migraine, headaches, high BP, etc. Ketu is detached from everything and a person sometimes loses interest in self-health. Rahu transit in the fourth house indicates an emotional imbalance, fear of the unknown, mental disturbances and heart issues.

This period 14 May to 18 Oct 2025, may be crucial as any problem arising during this period will not be diagnosed. Jupiter in the eighth house causes problems related to the digestive system such as the liver, kidneys, and weight gain or loss. Diabetes etc, if Jupiter is weak in the natal chart and the person is going period of Jupiter. Be mindful of your diet as it may increase, leading to weight-related health issues. Do not ignore any health-related warnings as visits to hospitals and expenditures are likely during that period. Jupiter is in the eighth house, potentially leading to medical expenditures.

Fasting on Thursdays or a day of your choice can be beneficial for health-related matters. Making changes in your eating habits, along with regular exercise and weekly fasting, can improve your overall well-being. Health should be a top priority, so ensure you follow through with medical check-ups as advised and stay proactive about your health.

From 13 July to 25 Nov 2025, there may be medical issues related to arms, legs, knees, and feet, especially for individuals with afflicted Saturn in their birth chart. They should be particularly cautious about their arms and legs during that period.

On 18 Oct 2025, Jupiter transits to the ninth house and provides you timely relief and protection from any chronic disease but minor health issues cannot be ruled out. Any long pending health issues will be recovered.

MONTH WISE PREDICTIONS

After going through predictions in general, let us find out certain periods where some changes will be expected. I wanted to be more specific but as there is no fixed pattern to consider the timelines, the best method was to take transit of the Sun, which takes approx 30 days, and then include the transit of other planets, during that period. Sun is the King of the Solar system. Sun being the heaviest and largest planet has the maximum effect on living organisms as compared to any other planet. If the Sun is in benefic state, it can counter the evil effects of any malefic planet. That may be the reason that I have given due importance to the transit of the Sun. However, an effort has been made to include the effect of conjunctions of planets during that period further helps to reach better accuracy. Major Planets such as Saturn, Rahu, Ketu, and Jupiter are going to transit for longer durations and affect the life path. But within that longer period, good or bad events will occur based on the transit of inner planets. I could only think of this as the best option. Your comments or feedback on this is always welcome to improve the procedures. This is in consideration of the transit of the Sun and other planets in general.

You should consider that these predictions are based on general planetary movement and do not consider the natal chart of individuals. Period, sub-period and planet position in the natal chart have major significance and vary from person to person and even twins have a lot of variations. It is better to consult an astrologer for a personalized annual horoscope. It does not cost much but gives you some psychological support and some warning for which you can take some precautions. Also, remember that there is no remedy for fixed or incurable Karmas as you have to face them in this life cycle or the next one.

Period: 01 Jan to 13 Jan 2025

The planetary position for the Scorpio sign on 01 Jan 2025, as the Sun is in transit in Sagittarius, will be as per the chart: -

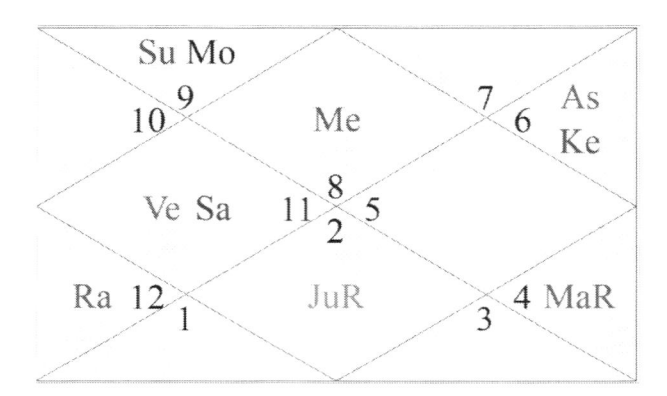

During this period, Sun transit in the second house, house of speech, family and finances will create a lot of opportunities or challenges regarding financial matters, such as inheritance, loans, debts, or joint ventures. Those having inheritance issues may find a positive outcome. Your communication skills will be appreciated by others and you will prove yourself as an eloquent speaker. You will get an opportunity to interact with your family members. Any of your family members may get an appreciation or recognition.

Sun is the planet of vitality and you may like to take charge of your life and make things happen. Due to the Sun intense energies, you can be arrogant and impulsive. You will be assertive, aggressive, ambitious, quick-tempered and impatient, but also very determined and goal-oriented. You will be very possessive about the materialistic items. Though you will gain in finances, your aggressive and forceful dealings with others may lead to financial disputes.

You may suffer from some eye problems due to the heat and energy emitted by the Sun. There is a possibility of some skin problems as well.

The period from 01 Jan to 13 Jan 2025, looks promising with positive prospects in various aspects of your life. However, due to retrograde Jupiter and Mars, the positive results would be reduced.

Period: 14 Jan to 12 Feb 2025

The planetary position for the Scorpio sign as of 14 Jan 2025 as the Sun transit in Capricorn, will be as under: -

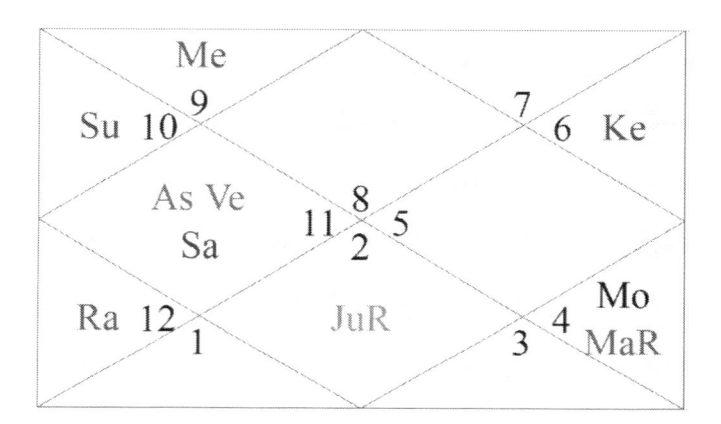

During this period, the focus area will be your profession, colleagues, siblings, short travels, and communications. You may feel more decisive and able to make quick decisions, especially concerning everyday matters.

During this period, the Sun aspected by Jupiter will transit in the third house, an upachay house in the Capricorn sign ruled by Saturn. The third house is associated with communication, short journeys, siblings, and skills. With the Sun transit in this house, you may have the opportunity to display effective communication and excel in roles that involve networking, negotiation, and conveying complex ideas with clarity. You will be successful in professions that demand precision, planning, and intellectual prowess. You will have a disciplined and practical energy combined with the Sun's vitality, creating a harmonious blend that fosters a strong work ethic, resilience, and a commitment to excellence. You may feel more decisive and able to make quick decisions, especially concerning everyday matters. It's a good time for reconnecting and resolving any communication issues. However, there may be some trouble getting along with your family members, especially your siblings which may be due to your ego issues.

You can expect a lot of positivity and numerous opportunities coming your way. You will be confident and ready to take on challenges and go after your goals. New opportunities will open, leading to growth in various aspects of your life. Your efforts may be recognized, and you could see success in your endeavors. People around you will look up to you for guidance and inspiration, and you might find yourself leading important projects. There may be gains in income, rise in position, overall happiness, recovery from disease, success in new ventures, association, and appreciation by the seniors. This period is associated with recognition by superiors, promotion and appreciation of the job.

Period: 13 Feb to 14 Mar 2025

The planetary position for Scorpio sign as of 13 Feb 2025, when the Sun transit to Aquarius will be as under: -

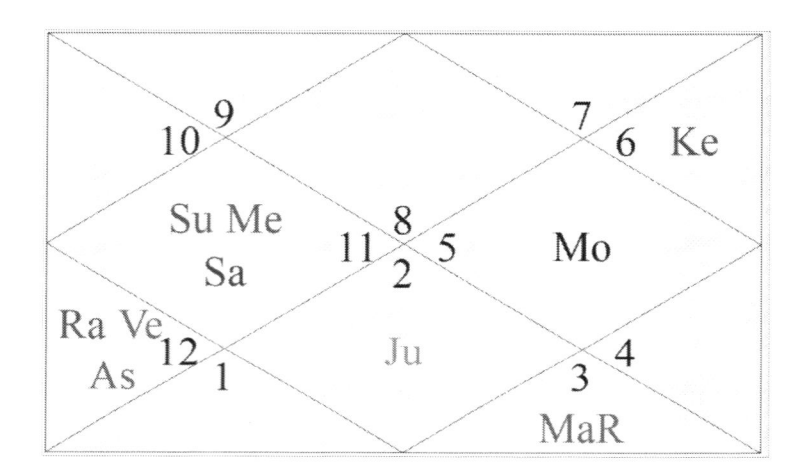

During this period Sun will transit over Saturn in the fourth house, which is not a favorable period. This conjunction is being formed in the Aquarius sign which is again a sign of social networking. Sun and Saturn are the extremes of the Solar system where the Sun represents the life force and Saturn signifies the end-of-life force. One radiates the energy and the other absorbs the entire energy as a black body. A similar effect can be observed here during this period, where you may have a contrast in requirements regarding family matters, health and Job pressure. There may be differences of opinion to extreme levels with the parents, higher authorities, government officials and even your father. Relations with your parents or the health of your mother may be an issue of concern for you. There might be some health issues to watch out for, and you may need to visit the hospital to be with someone you care about. It's essential to be mindful of your digestion and take care of your health by making positive changes to your diet and exercise habits. Despite your efforts at work, you may not receive the recognition you deserve. Nevertheless, you'll likely be more focused on being efficient and productive in your job and daily tasks. You might also find yourself dealing with and resolving conflicts or problems that come up at work or in your daily life. During this period, practical tasks and responsibilities will require your attention. You may feel a strong desire to help others and be kind to them. It's an excellent opportunity to organize your life and create a structured daily routine. Simplifying and decluttering your living and working spaces might also be on your mind during this time.

On the positive side, this period can be quite positive as the Sun and Saturn in the fourth house indicate that you are doing your duties toward your parents. Long pending property dispute may be resolved. During this time, you could be quite busy with your work and managing your daily routine and responsibilities. Those who want to buy or sell land or property may succeed in this period.

Period: 15 Mar to 13 Apr 2025

The planetary position for the Scorpio sign as of 15 Mar 2025, at the time Sun transit to Pisces will be as under:

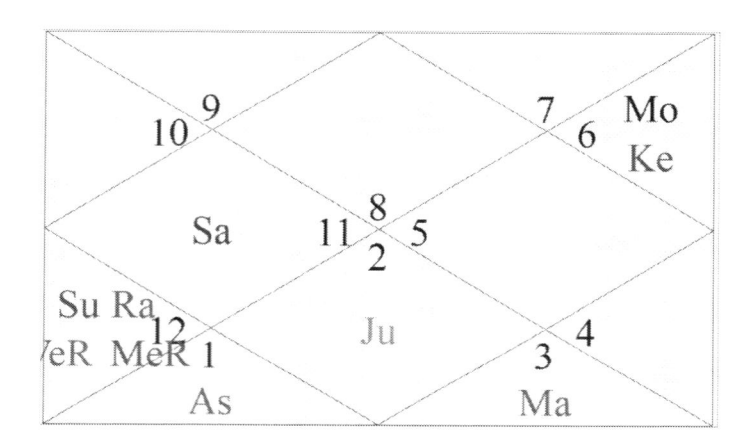

During this period, Saturn transits to Pisces on 29 Mar 2025 for 2 years and 2 months till 3 June 2027. This is a major transit when Sade Sati of Aries will commence and Capricorn will be free from Shani Sade Sati. Rahu transit to Aquarius and Ketu to Leo on 18 May 2025.

Conjunction: In Pisces, Rahu Venus, Mercury and Sun from 14 Mar to 29 Mar 2025. After Saturn's transit to Pisces on 29 Mar 2025, five planets Rahu, Saturn, Mercury, Venus and Sun will be in conjunction from 29 Mar to 14 Apr 2025. Kaal Sarp Yoga is being formed on 29 Mar 2025.

During this period, your primary emphasis will be on matters related to the implementation of your creative ideas, hobbies, children, education, relationships, partnerships, marriage, and one-to-one connections.

During this period, Sun will be in transit in the fifth house. Your creativity pursuits may re-emerge. You may find time to engage in artistic or expressive activities, pursuing hobbies, artistic endeavors, and activities that bring joy. If you have a flair for performing or public speaking, then you may get an opportunity to showcase your talents and that may boost your confidence.

This period encourages you to have fun and enjoy life. You might seek entertainment, engage in recreational activities, or attend social events that bring happiness. You may feel more adventurous and willing to step out of your comfort zone to pursue your passions. You may even go for an adventurous hike during this period.

Due to the Sun Rahu conjunction, you can get unexpected results which may be good or bad. Sun energies are expended without any control. On the positive side, it can give a great boost to your career. Those who are in politics may find this a great time when they may be able to influence the Public. On the negative side, there can be anger outbursts which can burn everything at a family or professional level. It can also cause health issues especially related to the heart. There could be an increased focus on romantic interactions, and you may feel more playful and spontaneous in your relationships. You could get involved in spending time with children, being more involved in their lives, or considering matters related to parenting.

You're expected to consider your significant relationships, including those with your spouse, romantic partner, or close business associates. You might feel more assertive in your relationships and try to dominate in your relationship. Due to Mercury and Venus retrograde, further Saturn joining the conjunction on 29 Mar 2025, there may be certain major challenges in the relationship.

You might be engaged in speculative ventures, such as investing or gambling. It's essential to exercise caution and not take excessive risks during this transit.

For some individuals, this transit might be related to matters of fertility, conception, or pregnancy. For students, this period can be quite positive and those who are looking to go abroad for higher studies may find success, but they will be struggling a lot for visas.

The period 15 Mar to 07 Apr 2025, as Mercury turns retrograde, the period may affect the results as perceived and bring challenges in your education, love relationships, speculations, finances, and inheritance. Avoid any major decisions related to family activities, marriage and investment during this retro period.

Kaal Sarp Yoga being formed from 29 Mar to 28 July 2025. Kaal Sarp Yoga may obstruct or delay the expected gains. Energies of Venus and Rahu may trigger powerful sexual desires or fantasies that could potentially lead them into inappropriate relationships. Be cautious as there's a possibility of revived health concerns, accidents, or unresolved matters. Previous unethical actions might also come back to haunt you. Restlessness and impulsivity might undermine your inner peace. Struggles or even serious disagreements with your spouse are likely. If you're married and facing problems, exercise extra caution during this period.

The Kaal Sarp Yoga is likely to affect the entire population at one level or another with varying intensity. I find this period will be quite challenging for the entire world, as all planets are under Kaal Sarp Yoga. Several unexpected activities or accidents may happen in different places in the world. Tension among the countries may increase and some countries may be on the verge of war.

Period: 14 Apr to 14 May 2025

The planetary position for the Scorpio sign as of 14 Apr 2025, at the time when the Sun transits to Aries will be as under: -

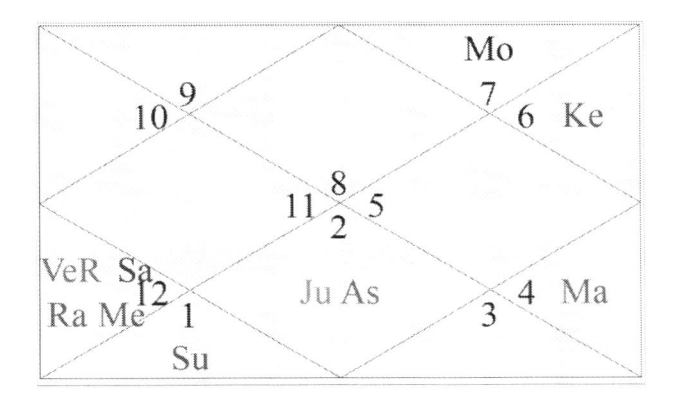

During this period, the Sun lord of the tenth house transit in the sixth house in its exaltation sign Aries. The Sixth House is Karma house and signifies Disease, enemies and debts.

This period is going to bestow you with a great time for the profession. You will overcome all your fears and will move with energy and confidence to achieve success in your life. It appears that your entire focus will be on your career and professional life. You could be quite busy with your work and managing your daily routine and responsibilities. You will be determined to meet your targets and dedicate yourself completely to your job. Your ambition and goal-oriented mindset will push you to efficiently complete any pending tasks. You may get the chance to showcase your leadership qualities by participating in important meetings, making crucial decisions, and guiding others. As a result, your public image and reputation are likely to improve, and people will admire and respect you for your achievements and contributions.

You would be victorious over your enemies and successful in competitions. Long pending issues, disputes or debts can be resolved. You will have success in financial matters. Any health issues, if troubling for a long or since last month may be cured. You will be bestowed with good health, good earnings and success in new ventures. You may get involved with charitable activities or with NGOs. This is a good time to focus on personal growth and becoming better at various aspects of your life.

You will get support from unexpected people who may be quite influential. Their support and motivation can bring you to the center stage. You can prove yourself as an authority in managing other people's finances. You will have a strong will and the ability to overcome difficult circumstances. You can harness your inner strength and vitality, even in the most challenging situations.

If you've been seeking new job opportunities, promotions, upgrades, or rewards, this period holds the potential for success in these areas. The stars seem to be favoring your career advancement, and you might find yourself in an influential position. So, embrace this positive phase and make the most of the opportunities that come your way in professional life.

Period: 15 May to 14 June 2025

The planetary position for the Scorpio sign on 15 May 2025, at the time Sun transit to Taurus will be as per the chart: -

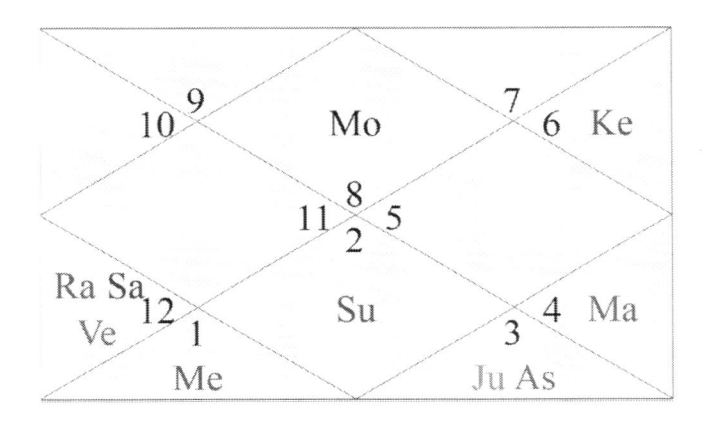

Sun will transit in the seventh house and possibly will give you mixed results. The seventh house signifies partnerships, marriage, your projection to others, creativity, and vitality. During this period, your sense of self and personal identity is closely tied to your relationships and partnerships. Your primary emphasis will be on matters related to relationships, partnerships, marriage, and one-to-one connections. You're expected to consider your significant relationships, including those with your spouse, romantic partner, or close business associates. If you are married, there may be some problems in your married life. You may struggle with finding a balance between your own needs and the needs of your partner. You may also experience power struggles or conflicts in your partnerships, as the Sun in the seventh house can indicate a need for control and dominance in relationships.

Sun is a separatist planet and its transit over the seventh house creates a lot of ego and anger issues resulting in disagreement with the life partner. Further, Venus in the sixth and Jupiter in the eighth house are not very positive for married life. Having undue expectations from a partner may create a rift so be practical and try to understand the problems of others. Those who tend to be cozy easily with opposite-sex friends are advised to remain in social and moral norms. It's advised to be cautious and avoid unnecessary arguments or conflicts with your life partner during this time to prevent any trouble.

Your social connections might be affected by your attitude, so it's essential to be mindful of how you interact with others. Take care of the health of your parents and your life partner during this period.

At the professional level, Sun transit in the seventh house and aspect over Lagna will boost your confidence and you can expect a lot of positivity and numerous opportunities coming your way. You will be ambitious and will have the courage to express yourself and lead others. You would like to explore and broaden your horizons.

Period: 15 June to 15 July 2025

The planetary position for Scorpio on 15 June 2025, at the time Sun transit to Gemini will be as per the chart: -

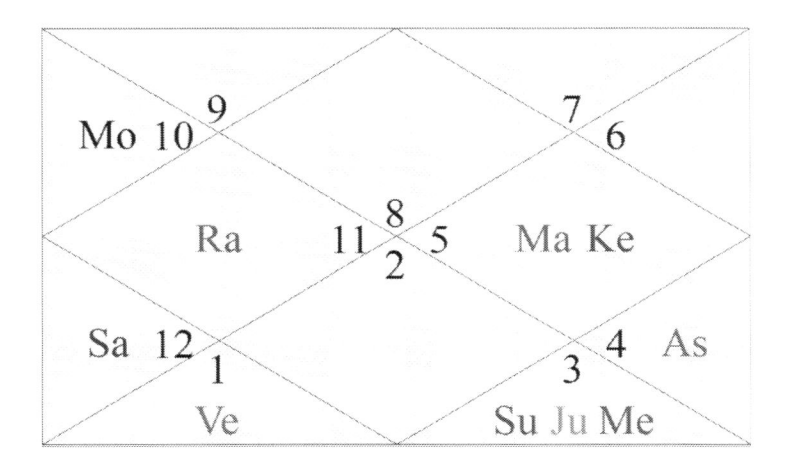

During this period, the Sun and Jupiter conjunct in the eighth house. The eighth house is associated with transformation, change, and rebirth, joint resources, shared values, and intimacy. You will experience transformation and growth through shared resources and intimate relationships.

There may be a mix of challenges and transformative potential, affecting areas such as personal growth, vitality, hidden matters, and spirituality. There can be sudden and profound changes in life, which can be both positive and negative. You are likely to experience significant transformation through crises or deep self-exploration. You can be interested in uncovering hidden truths, exploring the occult, and understanding the deeper aspects of life. This can manifest as an interest in astrology, tantra, or other mystical practices. You will have a strong desire to explore the deeper mysteries of life and will be drawn to spiritual or metaphysical practices.

You can have unexpected gains and breakthroughs. There can be sudden financial gains, inheritances, or windfalls. It may also lead to success in dealing with complex or hidden matters. You will be quite aware of your health issues and take all preventive measures to keep you fit and healthy by making necessary lifestyle changes. You will be able to effectively manage health conditions through disciplined efforts and transformation. Few Scorpio may adopt alternative therapies or spiritual practices for healing. You would like to keep your activities secretive. Your relationship with your father may be complex or strained.

You may be involved in home-related activities, such as renovating, redecorating, or making changes to your living space to enhance your comfort and well-being. There may be some family function family reunion or some auspicious activity. There may be a sudden gain of income or financial gain from any property or inheritance. You will be inclined to be generous and engage in charitable activities, supporting others especially your family members in need. There may be growth in the family or some family function for which you will be playing a major role as a responsible family member or as a sponsor for the function. You will have peace, comfort and happiness in the family and home. You should control your urge to dominate others and get too involved in activities at home front or with family. Let everyone in the family handle his role and responsibilities. You may get sudden travel opportunities, especially related to work or spiritual pursuits.

Saturn retrogradation from 13 July 2025 is likely to affect your relationship. Gains that you were expecting may not fructify easily or get delayed.

Period: 16 July to 16 Aug 2025

The planetary position for Scorpio on 16 July 2025, at the time Sun transit to Cancer will be as per the chart: -

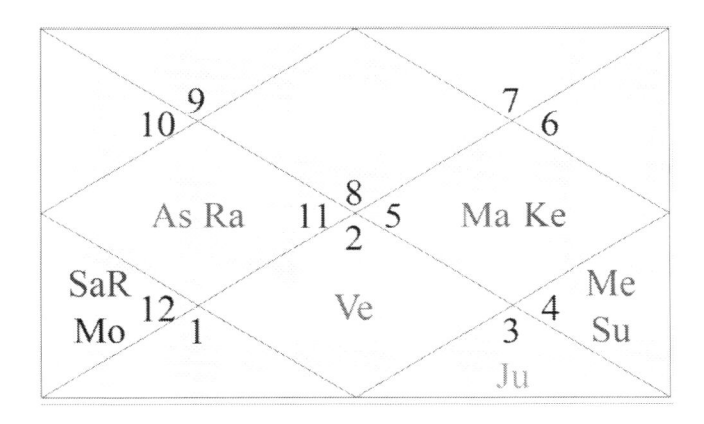

During this time, the Sun will be in transit in the ninth house, a house associated with religion, morality, higher education, legal matters, and father. This period brings a lot of positivity and many opportunities. Your confidence will increase, and you'll feel more optimistic about life. You'll have plenty of energy, making it a great time to take a trip, go on an adventure, or engage in activities that broaden your knowledge and understanding of the world. You might find yourself traveling frequently for business or adventure, with a strong urge to explore your surroundings. If your job involves travel, you could be required to visit distant or even foreign places. If you are not traveling anywhere, you can expect more interactions with people from other countries or different backgrounds. You need to be attentive to the health of your father.

You might feel inspired to study new subjects or pursue higher education. This is a particularly favorable time for students, who are likely to succeed. Your interest in spiritual matters and philosophical thinking might lead you to travel and connect with religious individuals.

You will experience happiness from your siblings and children, though having too many expectations from them could cause stress. Your siblings' health may also be a concern. You should not be arrogant with your seniors and father, as a stubborn and aggressive attitude could lead to conflicts with them. There could also be delays in acquiring the property that you've been planning.

After 18 July to 11 Aug 2025, Mercury will be retrograde, and Saturn will already be under retrogradation. You may find that you are not able to decide matter related to property. Renovation or dealing with property may keep your mind in confusion. You get in a dilemma about how to react in family and social relationships.

Period: 17 Aug to 16 Sep 2025

The planetary position for the Scorpio sign on 17 Aug 2025, at the time Sun transit to Leo will be as per the chart:

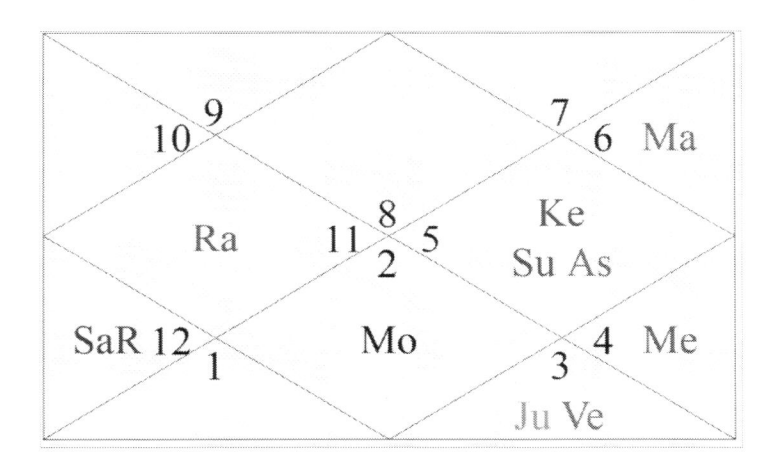

During this period, the Sun conjuncts Ketu in the tenth house, in the sign of Leo. The Sun, ruling Leo, represents ego, identity, and a sense of purpose, while Ketu signifies detachment, spirituality, and karmic release. On a positive note, this alignment can bring recognition, success in your professional life, and appreciation for your efforts.

However, with this conjunction in the tenth house, which governs career, reputation, and public standing, challenges may arise in maintaining a stable and prosperous professional path. There could be disruptions, unexpected changes, or a feeling of being misunderstood in your work or public life. The introspective, spiritual influence of Ketu might conflict with the Sun's drive for achievement and recognition, causing internal struggles between personal ambition and a desire for a more philosophical approach to life's work. On the positive side, any promotion or new job which you are expecting may fructify. There will be an improvement in financial status. You will be successful in all ventures that you are planning and making a sincere effort. You will benefit from your higher authorities, friends and relations. You may regain your lost position during this period.

During this period, you could be quite busy with your work and managing your daily routine and responsibilities. This is a good time to focus on personal growth and becoming better at various aspects of your life. Those who are looking for changing jobs or were not getting employment may find that new opportunities have emerged for them. Those who were waiting for increment, appreciation, promotion or recognition in their professional sphere may find the period is quite positive. If they are under the period of the Sun, Jupiter or Mars, chances are that they will get an upgrade in their profession.

On a material level, this conjunction may bring good fortune, wealth, and professional success. Stability and confidence could flourish in both your personal and professional life, making you comfortable with taking charge and initiating changes. You'll likely exhibit leadership qualities, handle financial matters more responsibly, and contribute innovative solutions to challenges. Improved communication and meaningful professional interactions are also likely.

You may experience a strong pull between craving success and recognition, yet feeling drawn to a simpler, less materialistic life. This internal conflict will require you to strike a balance between worldly ambitions and spiritual aspirations. The combined energies of the Sun and Ketu in the tenth house may trigger personal transformation and spiritual growth, often linked to a deeper connection with your ancestors and life purpose. It can foster wisdom and growth in both material and spiritual realms.

You may have issues with authority figures, superiors, or those in power may occur. Conflicts or a lack of support from leadership could hinder progress. To negate those challenges, you need to cultivate inner fulfillment, adopt a flexible mindset, and find ways to integrate your spiritual pursuits with your career goals.

Period: 17 Sep to 17 Oct 2025

The planetary position for the Scorpio sign on 17 Sep 2025, at the time Sun transit to Virgo will be as per the chart:

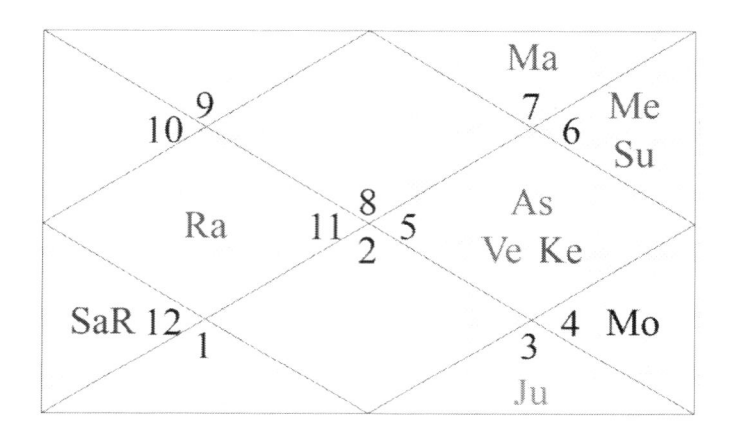

Sun will be in transit in the eleventh house. The eleventh house is the house of gains and social networks. This period will be a mix of your priorities regarding career and social networking. You may connect both and can have major gains in your profession. This is a positive time for career success, leadership, and positive social interactions. You will be ambitious and aggressive in your professional life but still tend to have a vast and diverse social network. You will be friendly, and outgoing, and enjoy being part of various groups and communities. People will be drawn towards you due to your charismatic and confident personality. You will have ambitious goals and dreams which you want to achieve. However, to achieve success you must work hard and also remain grounded and humble.

You may get a leadership role in social or professional groups and can be a motivating factor for others. You will tend to be involved in generosity and humanitarian causes and your activities may actively contribute to society and work for the betterment of others.

You will gain through contacts, friends, and social connections. Your contribution to society or hard work in professional life may attract others to You. You will get recognition for your participation in social activities, events, and gatherings.

Period: 18 Oct to 16 Nov 2025

The planetary position for the Scorpio sign on 18 Oct 2025, at the time Sun transit to Libra will be as per the chart:

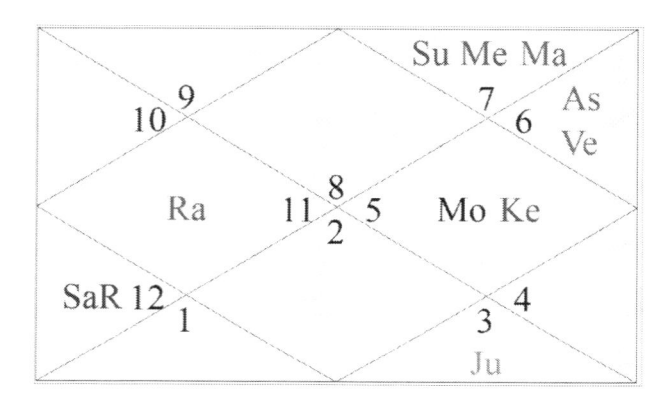

Sun and Mars will be in transit in the twelfth house and Jupiter will be in transit in the eighth house. This period will bring a lot of challenges, obstacles and roadblocks. The problems can manifest in the form of health, profession and married life. During this phase, there could be a noticeable depletion of life force and energy due \to health concerns affecting you or your family members, particularly your parents. This might necessitate visits to the hospital to care for your loved ones and manage associated expenses. Your interactions with siblings, colleagues, or your life partner might also become problematic during this time.

You need to be mindful of your anger and egoistic attitude at home and workplace. If your relations with your father are not good, then you may find the loss of happiness, obstacles in travel plans, loss of immovable property, fever, body pain and other diseases.

While you may possess a strong desire for recognition and admiration, you might struggle with expressing this openly. You may feel more comfortable working behind the scenes or supporting others from the shadows rather than seeking the spotlight for yourself. Your creative endeavors may be more personal and private, serving as a means of self-expression and purification. You may find comfort in retreating from the external world and spending time alone, where you can tap into your inner creativity and explore your depths.

You may have a deep longing to connect with something greater than yourself. You may find solace in spiritual practices, meditation, or exploring mystical and esoteric subjects. You will have a heightened sense of intuition and a strong connection to your subconscious mind.

You may be required to visit the hospital for eyesight issues. This might necessitate visits to the hospital for self-treatment or to care for your loved ones and manage associated expenses.

You may be traveling to a spiritual place or exploring a spiritual journey during this period. There can also be an opportunity to travel abroad for official work or leisure. Your employer may like to send you to negotiate a deal with any client.

Period: 17 Nov to 15 Dec 2025

The planetary position for the Scorpio sign on 17 Nov 2025, at the time Sun transit to Scorpio will be as per the chart: -

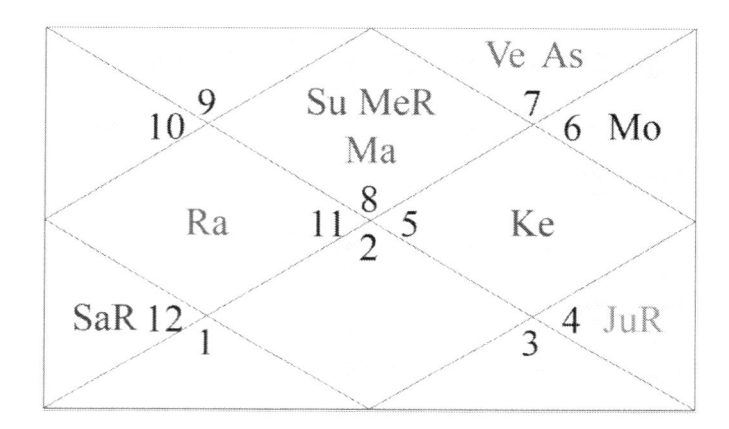

Sun, the Lagna Lord, in Lagna, brings the best of the time for the native. You can expect a lot of positivity and numerous opportunities coming your way. You will be confident, optimistic about life, energetic and full of energy. This positive outlook will make you eager to take on challenges and go after your goals. New opportunities will open, leading to growth in various aspects of your life. Your efforts may be recognized, and you could see success in your endeavors.

The period seems promising with positive prospects in various aspects of your life. There may be gains in income, rise in position, overall happiness, recovery from disease, success in new ventures, association, and appreciation by the seniors. This period is associated with recognition by superiors, promotion and appreciation of the job. Your focus area will be your profession, colleagues, short travels, and communications.

During this period, your primary emphasis will be on self-health, self-growth, matters related to relationships, partnerships, marriage, and one-to-one connections. You're expected to consider your significant relationships, including those with your spouse, romantic partner, or close business associates. Your attitude could create some challenges or conflicts with your life partner or business partner. On the professional front and for your social status, you may grow and can have major gains in your profession. This is a positive time for career success, leadership, and positive social interactions.

Due to your busy schedule or ego issues, your interests towards sexual interest will be lacking which further may affect your relationship with your life partner. If you are married, there may be some problems in your married life. It's advised to be cautious and avoid unnecessary arguments or conflicts with your life partner during this time to prevent any trouble. Sun and Mars will be in transit in the Lagna. Two separatist planets in the Lagna and Venus in the twelfth house are not a positive transit for married life. Having undue expectations from a partner may create a rift so be practical and try to understand the problems of others. Those who tend to be cozy easily with opposite-sex friends are advised to remain in social and moral norms.

Period: 16 Dec to 31 Dec 2025

The planetary position for the Scorpio sign on 16 Dec 2025, at the time Sun transit to Sagittarius will be as per the chart: -

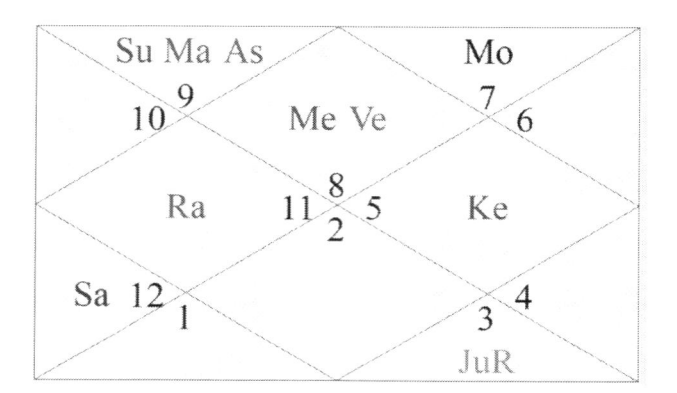

Sun transit in the second house, house of speech, family and finances will create a lot of opportunities or challenges regarding financial matters, such as inheritance, loans, debts, or joint ventures. Those having inheritance issues may find a positive outcome. Your communication skills will be appreciated by others and you will prove yourself as an eloquent speaker. You will get an opportunity to interact with your family members. Any of your family members may get an appreciation or recognition.

Sun is the planet of vitality and Mars is the planet of action. You may like to take charge of your life and make things happen. Due to the energies of two luminaries, you can be arrogant and impulsive. You may involve yourself in multiple projects and lose focus on one task or goal. You may be assertive, aggressive, ambitious, quick-tempered and impatient, but also very determined and goal-oriented. You will be very possessive about the materialistic items. You will gain in finances, however, you are aggressive and forceful in your dealings with others, which could lead to financial disputes.

You may suffer from some eye problems due to the heat and energy emitted by the Sun and Mars. There is a possibility of some skin problems as well.

PREDICTIONS BASED ON MOON TRANSIT

The journey of Annual Horoscope 2025, began with predictions based on the transit of major planets and then shifted to Solar movement, which could forecast events monthly.

The effect during the entire month cannot be the same as the Moon which passes through each sign in 2 1/4 days and covers 12 signs roughly in 30 days from birth sign (Janma Rasi) has major effects on happening in our life. However, to bring on almost daily, we will be going through predictions based on Moon transit and how the day will be today based on Moon transit in a particular Nakshatra.

Moon goes through a complete Zodiac in approx 30 days which means that he will be good for about 15 days in a month. The good results are not continuous but intermittent. During the same time, the other planets give either good or bad results. Though it will not be humanly possible to give effects of other planets here, I will be covering the predictions based on Moon transit in a particular house only.

In essence, understanding the nuances of Moon transits in astrology will give you an idea of what is going on in life, but the details that are given can differ in your chart because of different natal charts. Every chart carries a different promise and Dasha and Transit will deliver the promise as the event only.

In the first part of this chapter, I will be giving the tables indicating the period when the Moon transit in a sign along with the house number. You just need to check the date and house number. Go to the predictions given for that house number which are given in the next part of this chapter.

For example, if you want to check the period 23 Jan 2025 22:32 hrs to 26 Jan 2025 08:26 hrs, you will notice from ser No 11 at table "Table of Transit of Moon in Signs and Houses" below that the Moon is in transit in the Scorpio sign and will transit in the first house for the Scorpio sign. Go to "Moon Transit in the First House" for predictions.

Another example for 01 Apr 2025, ser No 41, Moon transit in Taurus sign and Seventh house for Scorpio. Go to Prediction for Moon transit in the Second house for results.

You will be going through the effects that you may observe in a span of 2 ¼ days. This will be based on Moon transit in a particular house of the chart. These predictions are generally quite accurate and help you to plan the activities.

In the second part of this chapter, "Day-wise Predictions", I will be going further into the period of each day of the year 2025. Those will be based on Nakshatra-based transit for the Moon. You should consider these predictions while doing any important activities. You need to check the date and time given in the table and events that may happen on that day. The charts are given to cover the dates of the entire year when the Moon transits over a particular Nakshatra.

No	Sign	From	To	House
1	Capricorn	01/01/2025 06:01	03/01/2025 10:47	3
2	Aquarius	03/01/2025 10:47	05/01/2025 14:34	4
3	Pisces	05/01/2025 14:34	07/01/2025 17:49	5
4	Aries	07/01/2025 17:49	09/01/2025 20:46	6
5	Taurus	09/01/2025 20:46	11/01/2025 23:55	7
6	Gemini	11/01/2025 23:55	14/01/2025 04:19	8
7	Cancer	14/01/2025 04:19	16/01/2025 11:16	9
8	Leo	16/01/2025 11:16	18/01/2025 21:28	10
9	Virgo	18/01/2025 21:28	21/01/2025 10:03	11
10	Libra	21/01/2025 10:03	23/01/2025 22:32	12
11	Scorpio	23/01/2025 22:32	26/01/2025 08:26	1
12	Sagittarius	26/01/2025 08:26	28/01/2025 14:51	2
13	Capricorn	28/01/2025 14:51	30/01/2025 18:34	3
14	Aquarius	30/01/2025 18:34	01/02/2025 20:58	4
15	Pisces	01/02/2025 20:58	03/02/2025 23:16	5
16	Aries	03/02/2025 23:16	06/02/2025 02:15	6
17	Taurus	06/02/2025 02:15	08/02/2025 06:21	7
18	Gemini	08/02/2025 06:21	10/02/2025 11:56	8
19	Cancer	10/02/2025 11:56	12/02/2025 19:35	9
20	Leo	12/02/2025 19:35	15/02/2025 05:44	10
21	Virgo	15/02/2025 05:44	17/02/2025 18:02	11
22	Libra	17/02/2025 18:02	20/02/2025 06:49	12
23	Scorpio	20/02/2025 06:49	22/02/2025 17:40	1
24	Sagittarius	22/02/2025 17:40	25/02/2025 00:55	2
25	Capricorn	25/02/2025 00:55	27/02/2025 04:36	3
26	Aquarius	27/02/2025 04:36	01/03/2025 05:57	4

No	Sign	From	To	House
27	Pisces	01/03/2025 05:57	03/03/2025 06:39	5
28	Aries	03/03/2025 06:39	05/03/2025 08:12	6
29	Taurus	05/03/2025 08:12	07/03/2025 11:45	7
30	Gemini	07/03/2025 11:45	09/03/2025 17:45	8
31	Cancer	09/03/2025 17:45	12/03/2025 02:15	9
32	Leo	12/03/2025 02:15	14/03/2025 12:56	10
33	Virgo	14/03/2025 12:56	17/03/2025 01:15	11
34	Libra	17/03/2025 01:15	19/03/2025 14:06	12
35	Scorpio	19/03/2025 14:06	22/03/2025 01:45	1
36	Sagittarius	22/03/2025 01:45	24/03/2025 10:24	2
37	Capricorn	24/03/2025 10:24	26/03/2025 15:14	3
38	Aquarius	26/03/2025 15:14	28/03/2025 16:47	4
39	Pisces	28/03/2025 16:47	30/03/2025 16:34	5
40	Aries	30/03/2025 16:34	01/04/2025 16:30	6
41	Taurus	01/04/2025 16:30	03/04/2025 18:21	7
42	Gemini	03/04/2025 18:21	05/04/2025 23:25	8
43	Cancer	05/04/2025 23:25	08/04/2025 07:54	9
44	Leo	08/04/2025 07:54	10/04/2025 19:04	10
45	Virgo	10/04/2025 19:04	13/04/2025 07:38	11
46	Libra	13/04/2025 07:38	15/04/2025 20:26	12
47	Scorpio	15/04/2025 20:26	18/04/2025 08:20	1
48	Sagittarius	18/04/2025 08:20	20/04/2025 18:04	2
49	Capricorn	20/04/2025 18:04	23/04/2025 00:31	3
50	Aquarius	23/04/2025 00:31	25/04/2025 03:25	4
51	Pisces	25/04/2025 03:25	27/04/2025 03:38	5
52	Aries	27/04/2025 03:38	29/04/2025 02:53	6
53	Taurus	29/04/2025 02:53	01/05/2025 03:14	7

No	Sign	From	To	House
54	Gemini	01/05/2025 03:14	03/05/2025 06:36	8
55	Cancer	03/05/2025 06:36	05/05/2025 14:01	9
56	Leo	05/05/2025 14:01	08/05/2025 00:57	10
57	Virgo	08/05/2025 00:57	10/05/2025 13:42	11
58	Libra	10/05/2025 13:42	13/05/2025 02:27	12
59	Scorpio	13/05/2025 02:27	15/05/2025 14:07	1
60	Sagittarius	15/05/2025 14:07	18/05/2025 00:03	2
61	Capricorn	18/05/2025 00:03	20/05/2025 07:35	3
62	Aquarius	20/05/2025 07:35	22/05/2025 12:08	4
63	Pisces	22/05/2025 12:08	24/05/2025 13:48	5
64	Aries	24/05/2025 13:48	26/05/2025 13:40	6
65	Taurus	26/05/2025 13:40	28/05/2025 13:36	7
66	Gemini	28/05/2025 13:36	30/05/2025 15:42	8
67	Cancer	30/05/2025 15:42	01/06/2025 21:36	9
68	Leo	01/06/2025 21:36	04/06/2025 07:35	10
69	Virgo	04/06/2025 07:35	06/06/2025 20:06	11
70	Libra	06/06/2025 20:06	09/06/2025 08:50	12
71	Scorpio	09/06/2025 08:50	11/06/2025 20:10	1
72	Sagittarius	11/06/2025 20:10	14/06/2025 05:38	2
73	Capricorn	14/06/2025 05:38	16/06/2025 13:09	3
74	Aquarius	16/06/2025 13:09	18/06/2025 18:35	4
75	Pisces	18/06/2025 18:35	20/06/2025 21:44	5
76	Aries	20/06/2025 21:44	22/06/2025 23:03	6
77	Taurus	22/06/2025 23:03	24/06/2025 23:45	7
78	Gemini	24/06/2025 23:45	27/06/2025 01:39	8
79	Cancer	27/06/2025 01:39	29/06/2025 06:34	9
80	Leo	29/06/2025 06:34	01/07/2025 15:23	10

No	Sign	From	To	House
81	Virgo	01/07/2025 15:23	04/07/2025 03:19	11
82	Libra	04/07/2025 03:19	06/07/2025 16:00	12
83	Scorpio	06/07/2025 16:00	09/07/2025 03:15	1
84	Sagittarius	09/07/2025 03:15	11/07/2025 12:08	2
85	Capricorn	11/07/2025 12:08	13/07/2025 18:53	3
86	Aquarius	13/07/2025 18:53	15/07/2025 23:58	4
87	Pisces	15/07/2025 23:58	18/07/2025 03:39	5
88	Aries	18/07/2025 03:39	20/07/2025 06:11	6
89	Taurus	20/07/2025 06:11	22/07/2025 08:14	7
90	Gemini	22/07/2025 08:14	24/07/2025 10:59	8
91	Cancer	24/07/2025 10:59	26/07/2025 15:52	9
92	Leo	26/07/2025 15:52	29/07/2025 00:00	10
93	Virgo	29/07/2025 00:00	31/07/2025 11:15	11
94	Libra	31/07/2025 11:15	02/08/2025 23:52	12
95	Scorpio	02/08/2025 23:52	05/08/2025 11:22	1
96	Sagittarius	05/08/2025 11:22	07/08/2025 20:11	2
97	Capricorn	07/08/2025 20:11	10/08/2025 02:11	3
98	Aquarius	10/08/2025 02:11	12/08/2025 06:10	4
99	Pisces	12/08/2025 06:10	14/08/2025 09:05	5
100	Aries	14/08/2025 09:05	16/08/2025 11:43	6
101	Taurus	16/08/2025 11:43	18/08/2025 14:40	7
102	Gemini	18/08/2025 14:40	20/08/2025 18:35	8
103	Cancer	20/08/2025 18:35	23/08/2025 00:16	9
104	Leo	23/08/2025 00:16	25/08/2025 08:28	10
105	Virgo	25/08/2025 08:28	27/08/2025 19:21	11
106	Libra	27/08/2025 19:21	30/08/2025 07:52	12
107	Scorpio	30/08/2025 07:52	01/09/2025 19:55	1

No	Sign	From	To	House
108	Sagittarius	01/09/2025 19:55	04/09/2025 05:21	2
109	Capricorn	04/09/2025 05:21	06/09/2025 11:21	3
110	Aquarius	06/09/2025 11:21	08/09/2025 14:29	4
111	Pisces	08/09/2025 14:29	10/09/2025 16:03	5
112	Aries	10/09/2025 16:03	12/09/2025 17:30	6
113	Taurus	12/09/2025 17:30	14/09/2025 20:03	7
114	Gemini	14/09/2025 20:03	17/09/2025 00:28	8
115	Cancer	17/09/2025 00:28	19/09/2025 07:05	9
116	Leo	19/09/2025 07:05	21/09/2025 15:57	10
117	Virgo	21/09/2025 15:57	24/09/2025 02:55	11
118	Libra	24/09/2025 02:55	26/09/2025 15:23	12
119	Scorpio	26/09/2025 15:23	29/09/2025 03:54	1
120	Sagittarius	29/09/2025 03:54	01/10/2025 14:27	2
121	Capricorn	01/10/2025 14:27	03/10/2025 21:27	3
122	Aquarius	03/10/2025 21:27	06/10/2025 00:45	4
123	Pisces	06/10/2025 00:45	08/10/2025 01:28	5
124	Aries	08/10/2025 01:28	10/10/2025 01:23	6
125	Taurus	10/10/2025 01:23	12/10/2025 02:24	7
126	Gemini	12/10/2025 02:24	14/10/2025 05:58	8
127	Cancer	14/10/2025 05:58	16/10/2025 12:42	9
128	Leo	16/10/2025 12:42	18/10/2025 22:11	10
129	Virgo	18/10/2025 22:11	21/10/2025 09:36	11
130	Libra	21/10/2025 09:36	23/10/2025 22:05	12
131	Scorpio	23/10/2025 22:05	26/10/2025 10:46	1
132	Sagittarius	26/10/2025 10:46	28/10/2025 22:14	2
133	Capricorn	28/10/2025 22:14	31/10/2025 06:48	3
134	Aquarius	31/10/2025 06:48	02/11/2025 11:27	4

No	Sign	From	To	House
135	Pisces	02/11/2025 11:27	04/11/2025 12:34	5
136	Aries	04/11/2025 12:34	06/11/2025 11:46	6
137	Taurus	06/11/2025 11:46	08/11/2025 11:14	7
138	Gemini	08/11/2025 11:14	10/11/2025 13:03	8
139	Cancer	10/11/2025 13:03	12/11/2025 18:35	9
140	Leo	12/11/2025 18:35	15/11/2025 03:51	10
141	Virgo	15/11/2025 03:51	17/11/2025 15:35	11
142	Libra	17/11/2025 15:35	20/11/2025 04:13	12
143	Scorpio	20/11/2025 04:13	22/11/2025 16:46	1
144	Sagittarius	22/11/2025 16:46	25/11/2025 04:26	2
145	Capricorn	25/11/2025 04:26	27/11/2025 14:07	3
146	Aquarius	27/11/2025 14:07	29/11/2025 20:33	4
147	Pisces	29/11/2025 20:33	01/12/2025 23:18	5
148	Aries	01/12/2025 23:18	03/12/2025 23:14	6
149	Taurus	03/12/2025 23:14	05/12/2025 22:15	7
150	Gemini	05/12/2025 22:15	07/12/2025 22:38	8
151	Cancer	07/12/2025 22:38	10/12/2025 02:22	9
152	Leo	10/12/2025 02:22	12/12/2025 10:20	10
153	Virgo	12/12/2025 10:20	14/12/2025 21:41	11
154	Libra	14/12/2025 21:41	17/12/2025 10:26	12
155	Scorpio	17/12/2025 10:26	19/12/2025 22:51	1
156	Sagittarius	19/12/2025 22:51	22/12/2025 10:06	2
157	Capricorn	22/12/2025 10:06	24/12/2025 19:46	3
158	Aquarius	24/12/2025 19:46	27/12/2025 03:10	4
159	Pisces	27/12/2025 03:10	29/12/2025 07:40	5
160	Aries	29/12/2025 07:40	31/12/2025 09:23	6
161	Taurus	31/12/2025 09:23	02/01/2026 09:25	7

Moon in First House

This period promises comfort and luxury. You may purchase high-end items or vehicles and have opportunities to interact with people of higher status. Your good work may be appreciated by your seniors, leading to satisfaction with your performance and achieved results. It is a favorable time for progeny and learning Tantra and Mantras. Travel opportunities might arise, offering new learning experiences. You will enjoy good company, food, and other luxuries, and find satisfaction in family life, including sexual pleasure. A sense of contentment and self-assurance will often envelop you.

Financially, this period is favorable. You will easily recover dues and achieve your financial goals. Your married life will improve, enhancing your relationship with your spouse. It's a great time to enjoy with friends and acquaintances, particularly with the opposite sex. You and your family will experience good health without physical ailments. However, sometimes unstable thoughts may cause problems.

Moon in the Second House

This period may bring certain challenges on the financial and professional fronts. You might face fears of punishment from the government, such as paying late fees for bills or traffic fines. Despite your best efforts, your seniors may not agree with your suggestions or be satisfied with your performance. Your colleagues might avoid you and fail to cooperate, leading to unwanted expenditures. It is crucial to avoid impulsive spending and risky investments during this time.

Disagreements and quarrels with your spouse and friends are likely, so it's best to avoid arguments in all areas of life. You may feel frustration and discontentment. Eye problems may arise, and it is advisable to avoid traveling. Meditation could help alleviate the mental and physical fatigue associated with this period. Remember, these challenges will only last for a short time.

Moon in The Third House

This period promises mental peace, happiness, comfort, and satisfaction from all sides. You may receive good news within the family and find time to spend with your children. Self-confidence will help you face life's challenges. Your spouse will be cooperative, enhancing your enjoyment of intimate moments. Your siblings will prosper and succeed, and all your endeavors will be successful. Financially, you will see money coming from multiple sources, and your relationships with your spouse, neighbors, and relatives, especially younger siblings, will be strong.

You will have the courage to overcome obstacles and foster stronger bonds with friends and siblings. Your health will improve, and you will achieve significant success in your profession, meeting your desired goals. Your work will be appreciated, recognized, and rewarded by your superiors. This period will also be very rewarding financially, allowing you to recover past dues and gain well in all financial ventures. It is a good time for short-distance travel.

Overall, you will be happy and satisfied with life, enjoying everything that comes your way.

Moon in the Fourth House

There will be no peace at home. You will be in general unhappy and will not be able to enjoy due to mental or health issues. A sense of restlessness, grief, fear and doubt will prevail. Try your best to keep your cool and do not lose your mental balance. There will be a lack of comfort and mental peace. If the body constitution is weak, stomach pain, dysentery, digestive disorders and chest problems may come up. Drive carefully as it is an accident-prone period.

This will be a bad period for the mother as she may suffer bad health. Expenditures will increase. You may find impediments in work. You must be very careful with your investment ventures as it is a period of losses.

Relations will be sore and there will be a lack of understanding. There will be trouble from relatives, especially the ones from your mother's side. Avoid clashes and hostility. Some of your relatives may suffer loss of wealth and this may cause grief to you.

The time is not suitable for traveling. If forced to travel take double care of your health and expenses.

Moon in the Fifth House

During this period, issues concerning your children will take center stage. You will need to pay close attention to their health, emotions, and studies. Professionally, you will have to work harder to prove your competence and maintain your reputation. Meeting targets may be challenging due to various obstacles. If you are an investor or deal in financial markets, exercise caution.

Support from friends, colleagues, and even loved ones may be lacking. Be mindful of your food habits. Travel may present obstructions and risks of accidents, so take extra precautions. There will be wasteful expenditures, so take care of your belongings and avoid unnecessary spending.

Moon in the Sixth House

The period will be excellent as you will be able to handle your affairs confidently. There will be all-round improvement. There will be comfort during travel. You may get an opportunity to connect and liaise with new friends especially females and will enjoy their company.

You will be in an energetic and enthusiastic mood and will work comfortably at a fast pace. You will get victory over your enemies and competitors and will be successful in finishing the stuck-up undertakings. You will get good recognition and rewards from the bosses. Financially it is a very good period of gains and investments will yield good returns.

This period brings with it a ray of hope and auspicious outcomes. Success in efforts again, domestic harmony, and victory over adversaries are indicated during this period, instilling a sense of confidence and stability in natives.

Moon in the Seventh House

This period will be excellent, allowing you to handle your affairs with confidence. You will see overall improvement and comfort, especially during travel. You will have opportunities to meet and connect with new friends, particularly women, and will enjoy their company.

You will feel energetic and enthusiastic, working quickly and comfortably. You will defeat your enemies and competitors, and successfully finish any pending tasks. Your efforts will be recognized and rewarded by your bosses. Financially, this is a very good time, with gains and profitable returns on investments.

This period brings hope and positive outcomes. You will succeed in your efforts, enjoy harmony at home, and overcome adversaries, leading to confidence and stability.

Moon in the Eighth House

This period brings a lot of problems, obstacles and suffering. There will be many obstacles in your path at your workplace. Avoid conflicts and disagreements with your seniors. Do not indulge in secret dealings or scheming. Your enemies will increase and will give you trouble. Money will not come on time. Avoid all investments as it is a very bad period and the possibility of losses is very strong.

The mind is diverted to follow the wrong practices. Due to pressure from your spouse, you may get into enmity with others. There will be quarrels and disagreements at home. Married life will suffer. You may be thinking of evil about others and that attitude may result in hardship for you.

Unnecessary fear and anxiety, a sense of loss and gloom will prevail. A very bad time for health. Be careful while crossing the road and avoid all games, sports and activities involving physical risk. Avoid traveling as it is a very bad period for accidents and calamities.

Moon in the Ninth House

This period will bring positive results in all respects. You may feel drawn to spirituality and wish to visit a religious place. The time will be good for your wife and children, and you might experience a heightened temptation towards sex. Your humanitarian and charitable activities will be recognized. You will enjoy luxuries and travel. However, it is important to avoid disagreements or fights with your father.

Moon in the Tenth House

This is a very good time professionally. Your work will yield desirable results and earn the appreciation of your bosses. A promotion or honor is likely. Financially, this period is rewarding, making it an excellent time to start new projects. Money will come when needed, and investments will yield good returns.

Your family life will be happy and contented, with good conjugal bliss and a satisfying social life. You will gain a good reputation and respect in society. You may also need to travel for professional reasons.

Moon in the Eleventh House

During this period, you will experience good progress at work and will be supported by your friends, spouse, and seniors. Your bosses will respect and appreciate your efforts, and you may receive rewards. It's an excellent time for financial gains, with a boost in income and the ability to recover old dues. All financial investments will be fruitful, yielding very good returns.

On a personal level, this period brings happiness, joy, and a harmonious conjugal life. Your children will be affectionate and bring you happiness. You will make new friends and enjoy the company of the opposite sex. Your social life will be active with family reunions and gatherings with friends. Eligible individuals may even meet their future spouse.

You will enjoy worldly comforts, and your mood will be upbeat with a sense of delight and happiness. This is an auspicious time for travel, especially long-distance air travel, which will be fruitful and enjoyable.

Moon in the Twelfth House

During this period, you may face struggles and encounter obstacles. Your mind will be troubled by worries and fears, making it difficult to achieve desired targets despite your hard work. Your efforts may go unappreciated by your seniors. It's crucial to avoid underhand dealings and illegal activities. Instead of seeking progress and prosperity, focus on damage control to preserve your mental, physical, and financial resources.

There will be increased expenditure and insufficient income, leading to financial losses in various ways. Avoid all financial investments and transactions as this is a period prone to losses.

On a personal level, avoid arguments and conflicts with your spouse and relatives. Love and marital life may face challenges during this time. Avoid unnecessary travels as they may not be fruitful.

Your mental peace will be disturbed, and you may feel uneasy. However, you may find friendship with individuals outside your usual circle.

DAY WISE PREDICTIONS

After going through the predictions for 2 ¼ days, I would like to cover predictions for each day in the year 2025. How will be the day today? How will be my mood, progress, health, and finances for the day? I will be covering the daily predictions based on the transit of the Moon over the Nakshatras. Since I cannot differentiate the Sign-based predictions from Nakshatra-based events you are required to check your Nakshatra of Moon.

Moon will transit through the same nakshatras after every 27 days but you don't see repetition of events in your life after every 27 days. That will be due to other factors such as Dasha, Antar Dasha and the planetary position of other planets. However, the general effects will remain in the same pattern.

How to Check the Daily Predictions

The simple means is to check Moon Nakshatra from your birth chart or check the degrees of your Moon in the Scorpio sign. For the Scorpio sign, the Moon can be in the last one pada of Vishakha (16), four padas of Anuradha (17) and four padas of Jyeshta (18) Nakshatras. You can also check the Nakshatra from your birth chart as per the table below. The symbol has been given in front of that Nakshatra for relating to the "Transit of Moon in Nakshatras" and further result in "Result of Moon Transit as per Tara Bala".

Nakshatras in Scorpio Sign

S.No	Moon deg in Scorpio	Nakshatra	Nakshatra Seq
1	0 to 3.20 deg	Vishakha (16)	16 -X
2	3.20 to 16.40 deg	Anuradha (17)	17 - Y
2	16.40 to 30 deg	Jyeshta (18)	18 - Z

Further, for the timelines, I have given Moon transit in Nakshatra for each month for the entire year 2025. You have to check the sequence in front of the date from the monthly transit chart below as per your Birth Nakshatra and read the results given below in the heading "Result of Moon Transit as per Tara Bala".

Let us say your Birth Nakshatra is Vishakha (16) and you want to check for the date 5 Jan 2025. Since Vishakha is the first Nakshatra of Scorpio sign then it is X.

We go to the Jan 2025 chart and at **Ser No 5,** the Moon is in transit in the Purav Bhadapada (25) period given is 4 Jan 21:23 to 05 Jan 20:17. The Number in the line of **X** is given 1. It means the Moon is in transit over Birth Nakshatra for Vishakha (16). We go to the **"Results of Moon Transit as Per Tara Bala"** Ser No 1. It says" 1.   **Mixed results with both auspicious and inauspicious events. An average day**." So, this period is going to be mixed.

Now the period **5 Jan 20:17 to 06 Jan 2025 19:06** at **Ser No 6,** Moon is in transit in Uttar Bhadarpada (26) Nakshatra. **Against column X, it mentions 2 which means it will transit over the second Nakshtra from Birth Nakshtra, Vishakha (16).** As per result sheet Ser No 2, it is "2.   **A good period brings wealth, prosperity, enjoyment, and good fortune. Happiness in the family**.". So, this period will be good.

Let us say your Birth Nakshatra is Anuradha (17) and you want to check for the date 5 Jan 2025. Since Anuradha is the second

Nakshatra of Scorpio sign then it is **Y.**

We go to the Jan 2025 chart and at **Ser No 5,** the Moon is in transit in the Purav Bhadapada (25) period given is **4 Jan 21:23 to 05 Jan 20:17**. The Number in the line of **Y** is given 9. It means the Moon is in transit over Ati Mitra Nakshatra for Vishakha (16). We go to the **"Results of Moon Transit as Per Tara Bala"** Ser No 9. It says" **9.**
Very good results with gains and highly auspicious events. Gains through friends, alliances, and overall positive outcomes." So, this period is going to be excellent for Anuradha Nakshatra.

Let us say your Birth Nakshatra is Jyeshta (18) and you want to check for the date 10 Feb 2025. Since Jyestha (19) is the third Nakshatra of Scorpio sign then it is Z.

Now the period 10 Jan 13:45 to 11 Jan 12:29 is given at **Ser No 11** mentions number 5 in Column Z. Moon is in transit in Rohini (4) Nakshatra. The number **5** means Moon is in Praytri Nakshatra as per Tara Bala for Jyestha (18) Nakshatra. We go to the **"Results of Moon Transit as Per Tara Bala"** As per result sheet Ser No 5, it is **"5.**
Obstacles in all spheres of life, with obstructions, delays, and difficulties.". So, this period will be having problems.

Similarly, to check the day prediction, you may choose the day, your Nakshatra and Result sequence No. Check the result from the "Result of Moon Transit as per Tara Bala".

Results of Moon Transit as Per Tara Bala

1. Mixed results with both auspicious and inauspicious events. An average day.

2. A good period brings wealth, prosperity, enjoyment, and good fortune. Happiness in the family.

3. A struggleful period with inauspicious results, crises, dangers, obstacles, and challenges on the material level.

4. Good results in terms of prosperity, well-being, and increased fortune. Overall prosperity, security, stability, and well-being.

5. Obstacles in all spheres of life, with obstructions, delays, and difficulties.

6. Achievements, accomplishments, successes, and fulfillment of goals. Achievement of desires through sincere efforts.

7. A struggle period with inauspicious results, obstacles, dangers, severe misfortunes, troubles, illness, or loss.

8. A good period with happiness, companionship, support from friends, and gains through cooperation, and support.

9. Very good results with gains and highly auspicious events. Gains through friends, alliances, and overall positive outcomes.

Transit of Moon in Nakshatra: 01 Jan to 13 Jan 2025

SN	NK	Date Entry	Date Exit	X	Y	Z
1	21	01/01/2025 00:03	01/01/2025 23:45	6	5	4
2	22	01/01/2025 23:45	02/01/2025 23:10	7	6	5
3	23	02/01/2025 23:10	03/01/2025 22:21	8	7	6
4	24	03/01/2025 22:21	04/01/2025 21:23	9	8	7
5	25	04/01/2025 21:23	05/01/2025 20:17	1	9	8
6	26	05/01/2025 20:17	06/01/2025 19:06	2	1	9
7	27	06/01/2025 19:06	07/01/2025 17:49	3	2	1
8	1	07/01/2025 17:49	08/01/2025 16:29	4	3	2
9	2	08/01/2025 16:29	09/01/2025 15:06	5	4	3
10	3	09/01/2025 15:06	10/01/2025 13:45	6	5	4
11	4	10/01/2025 13:45	11/01/2025 12:29	7	6	5
12	5	11/01/2025 12:29	12/01/2025 11:24	8	7	6
13	6	12/01/2025 11:24	13/01/2025 10:37	9	8	7
14	7	13/01/2025 10:37	14/01/2025 10:16	1	9	8

Transit of Moon in Nakshatra: 14 Jan to 12 Feb 2025

SN	NK	Date Entry	Date Exit	X	Y	Z
15	8	14/01/2025 10:16	15/01/2025 10:27	2	1	9
16	9	15/01/2025 10:27	16/01/2025 11:16	3	2	1
17	10	16/01/2025 11:16	17/01/2025 12:44	4	3	2
18	11	17/01/2025 12:44	18/01/2025 14:51	5	4	3
19	12	18/01/2025 14:51	19/01/2025 17:29	6	5	4
20	13	19/01/2025 17:29	20/01/2025 20:29	7	6	5
21	14	20/01/2025 20:29	21/01/2025 23:36	8	7	6
22	15	21/01/2025 23:36	23/01/2025 02:34	9	8	7
23	16	23/01/2025 02:34	24/01/2025 05:08	1	9	8
24	17	24/01/2025 05:08	25/01/2025 07:07	2	1	9
25	18	25/01/2025 07:07	26/01/2025 08:25	3	2	1
26	19	26/01/2025 08:25	27/01/2025 09:01	4	3	2
27	20	27/01/2025 09:01	28/01/2025 08:58	5	4	3
28	21	28/01/2025 08:58	29/01/2025 08:20	6	5	4
29	22	29/01/2025 08:20	30/01/2025 07:14	7	6	5
30	23	30/01/2025 07:14	31/01/2025 05:50	8	7	6
31	24	31/01/2025 05:50	01/02/2025 04:14	9	8	7
32	25	01/02/2025 04:14	02/02/2025 02:32	1	9	8
33	26	02/02/2025 02:32	03/02/2025 00:51	2	1	9
34	27	03/02/2025 00:51	03/02/2025 23:16	3	2	1
35	1	03/02/2025 23:16	04/02/2025 21:49	4	3	2
36	2	04/02/2025 21:49	05/02/2025 20:32	5	4	3
37	3	05/02/2025 20:32	06/02/2025 19:29	6	5	4
38	4	06/02/2025 19:29	07/02/2025 18:39	7	6	5
39	5	07/02/2025 18:39	08/02/2025 18:06	8	7	6
40	6	08/02/2025 18:06	09/02/2025 17:52	9	8	7
41	7	09/02/2025 17:52	10/02/2025 18:00	1	9	8
42	8	10/02/2025 18:00	11/02/2025 18:33	2	1	9
43	9	11/02/2025 18:33	12/02/2025 19:35	3	2	1
44	10	12/02/2025 19:35	13/02/2025 21:06	4	3	2

SN	NK	Date Entry	Date Exit	X	Y	Z
		Transit of Moon in Nakshatra: 13 Feb to 13 Mar 2025				
45	11	13/02/2025 21:06	14/02/2025 23:09	5	4	3
46	12	14/02/2025 23:09	16/02/2025 01:39	6	5	4
47	13	16/02/2025 01:39	17/02/2025 04:31	7	6	5
48	14	17/02/2025 04:31	18/02/2025 07:35	8	7	6
49	15	18/02/2025 07:35	19/02/2025 10:39	9	8	7
50	16	19/02/2025 10:39	20/02/2025 13:30	1	9	8
51	17	20/02/2025 13:30	21/02/2025 15:53	2	1	9
52	18	21/02/2025 15:53	22/02/2025 17:40	3	2	1
53	19	22/02/2025 17:40	23/02/2025 18:42	4	3	2
54	20	23/02/2025 18:42	24/02/2025 18:58	5	4	3
55	21	24/02/2025 18:58	25/02/2025 18:30	6	5	4
56	22	25/02/2025 18:30	26/02/2025 17:23	7	6	5
57	23	26/02/2025 17:23	27/02/2025 15:43	8	7	6
58	24	27/02/2025 15:43	28/02/2025 13:40	9	8	7
59	25	28/02/2025 13:40	01/03/2025 11:22	1	9	8
60	26	01/03/2025 11:22	02/03/2025 08:59	2	1	9
61	27	02/03/2025 08:59	03/03/2025 06:38	3	2	1
62	1	03/03/2025 06:38	04/03/2025 04:29	4	3	2
63	2	04/03/2025 04:29	05/03/2025 02:37	5	4	3
64	3	05/03/2025 02:37	06/03/2025 01:08	6	5	4
65	4	06/03/2025 01:08	07/03/2025 00:05	7	6	5
66	5	07/03/2025 00:05	07/03/2025 23:31	8	7	6
67	6	07/03/2025 23:31	08/03/2025 23:28	9	8	7
68	7	08/03/2025 23:28	09/03/2025 23:54	1	9	8
69	8	09/03/2025 23:54	11/03/2025 00:51	2	1	9
70	9	11/03/2025 00:51	12/03/2025 02:15	3	2	1
71	10	12/03/2025 02:15	13/03/2025 04:05	4	3	2
72	11	13/03/2025 04:05	14/03/2025 06:19	5	4	3

Transit of Moon in Nakshatra: 14 Mar to 13 Apr 2025

SN	NK	Date Entry	Date Exit	X	Y	Z
73	12	14/03/2025 06:19	15/03/2025 08:53	6	5	4
74	13	15/03/2025 08:53	16/03/2025 11:45	7	6	5
75	14	16/03/2025 11:45	17/03/2025 14:46	8	7	6
76	15	17/03/2025 14:46	18/03/2025 17:51	9	8	7
77	16	18/03/2025 17:51	19/03/2025 20:49	1	9	8
78	17	19/03/2025 20:49	20/03/2025 23:31	2	1	9
79	18	20/03/2025 23:31	22/03/2025 01:45	3	2	1
80	19	22/03/2025 01:45	23/03/2025 03:23	4	3	2
81	20	23/03/2025 03:23	24/03/2025 04:18	5	4	3
82	21	24/03/2025 04:18	25/03/2025 04:26	6	5	4
83	22	25/03/2025 04:26	26/03/2025 03:49	7	6	5
84	23	26/03/2025 03:49	27/03/2025 02:29	8	7	6
85	24	27/03/2025 02:29	28/03/2025 00:33	9	8	7
86	25	28/03/2025 00:33	28/03/2025 22:09	1	9	8
87	26	28/03/2025 22:09	29/03/2025 19:26	2	1	9
88	27	29/03/2025 19:26	30/03/2025 16:34	3	2	1
89	1	30/03/2025 16:34	31/03/2025 13:44	4	3	2
90	2	31/03/2025 13:44	01/04/2025 11:06	5	4	3
91	3	01/04/2025 11:06	02/04/2025 08:49	6	5	4
92	4	02/04/2025 08:49	03/04/2025 07:02	7	6	5
93	5	03/04/2025 07:02	04/04/2025 05:50	8	7	6
94	6	04/04/2025 05:50	05/04/2025 05:20	9	8	7
95	7	05/04/2025 05:20	06/04/2025 05:31	1	9	8
96	8	06/04/2025 05:31	07/04/2025 06:24	2	1	9
97	9	07/04/2025 06:24	08/04/2025 07:54	3	2	1
98	10	08/04/2025 07:54	09/04/2025 09:56	4	3	2
99	11	09/04/2025 09:56	10/04/2025 12:24	5	4	3
100	12	10/04/2025 12:24	11/04/2025 15:10	6	5	4
101	13	11/04/2025 15:10	12/04/2025 18:07	7	6	5
102	14	12/04/2025 18:07	13/04/2025 21:10	8	7	6
103	15	13/04/2025 21:10	15/04/2025 00:13	9	8	7

SN	NK	Date Entry	Date Exit	X	Y	Z
		Transit of Moon in Nakshatra: 14 Apr to 14 May 2025				
104	16	15/04/2025 00:13	16/04/2025 03:10	1	9	8
105	17	16/04/2025 03:10	17/04/2025 05:54	2	1	9
106	18	17/04/2025 05:54	18/04/2025 08:20	3	2	1
107	19	18/04/2025 08:20	19/04/2025 10:20	4	3	2
108	20	19/04/2025 10:20	20/04/2025 11:48	5	4	3
109	21	20/04/2025 11:48	21/04/2025 12:36	6	5	4
110	22	21/04/2025 12:36	22/04/2025 12:43	7	6	5
111	23	22/04/2025 12:43	23/04/2025 12:07	8	7	6
112	24	23/04/2025 12:07	24/04/2025 10:49	9	8	7
113	25	24/04/2025 10:49	25/04/2025 08:53	1	9	8
114	26	25/04/2025 08:53	26/04/2025 06:27	2	1	9
115	27	26/04/2025 06:27	27/04/2025 03:38	3	2	1
116	1	27/04/2025 03:38	28/04/2025 00:38	4	3	2
117	2	28/04/2025 00:38	28/04/2025 21:37	5	4	3
118	3	28/04/2025 21:37	29/04/2025 18:46	6	5	4
119	4	29/04/2025 18:46	30/04/2025 16:17	7	6	5
120	5	30/04/2025 16:17	01/05/2025 14:20	8	7	6
121	6	01/05/2025 14:20	02/05/2025 13:03	9	8	7
122	7	02/05/2025 13:03	03/05/2025 12:33	1	9	8
123	8	03/05/2025 12:33	04/05/2025 12:53	2	1	9
124	9	04/05/2025 12:53	05/05/2025 14:01	3	2	1
125	10	05/05/2025 14:01	06/05/2025 15:51	4	3	2
126	11	06/05/2025 15:51	07/05/2025 18:16	5	4	3
127	12	07/05/2025 18:16	08/05/2025 21:06	6	5	4
128	13	08/05/2025 21:06	10/05/2025 00:08	7	6	5
129	14	10/05/2025 00:08	11/05/2025 03:15	8	7	6
130	15	11/05/2025 03:15	12/05/2025 06:17	9	8	7
131	16	12/05/2025 06:17	13/05/2025 09:09	1	9	8
132	17	13/05/2025 09:09	14/05/2025 11:46	2	1	9
133	18	14/05/2025 11:46	15/05/2025 14:07	3	2	1

Transit of Moon in Nakshatra: 15 May to 14 June 2025

SN	NK	Date Entry	Date Exit	X	Y	Z
134	19	15/05/2025 14:07	16/05/2025 16:07	4	3	2
135	20	16/05/2025 16:07	17/05/2025 17:43	5	4	3
136	21	17/05/2025 17:43	18/05/2025 18:52	6	5	4
137	22	18/05/2025 18:52	19/05/2025 19:29	7	6	5
138	23	19/05/2025 19:29	20/05/2025 19:31	8	7	6
139	24	20/05/2025 19:31	21/05/2025 18:57	9	8	7
140	25	21/05/2025 18:57	22/05/2025 17:47	1	9	8
141	26	22/05/2025 17:47	23/05/2025 16:02	2	1	9
142	27	23/05/2025 16:02	24/05/2025 13:48	3	2	1
143	1	24/05/2025 13:48	25/05/2025 11:12	4	3	2
144	2	25/05/2025 11:12	26/05/2025 08:23	5	4	3
145	3	26/05/2025 08:23	27/05/2025 05:32	6	5	4
146	4	27/05/2025 05:32	28/05/2025 02:50	7	6	5
147	5	28/05/2025 02:50	29/05/2025 00:28	8	7	6
148	6	29/05/2025 00:28	29/05/2025 22:38	9	8	7
149	7	29/05/2025 22:38	30/05/2025 21:28	1	9	8
150	8	30/05/2025 21:28	31/05/2025 21:07	2	1	9
151	9	31/05/2025 21:07	01/06/2025 21:36	3	2	1
152	10	01/06/2025 21:36	02/06/2025 22:55	4	3	2
153	11	02/06/2025 22:55	04/06/2025 00:58	5	4	3
154	12	04/06/2025 00:58	05/06/2025 03:35	6	5	4
155	13	05/06/2025 03:35	06/06/2025 06:33	7	6	5
156	14	06/06/2025 06:33	07/06/2025 09:39	8	7	6
157	15	07/06/2025 09:39	08/06/2025 12:41	9	8	7
158	16	08/06/2025 12:41	09/06/2025 15:30	1	9	8
159	17	09/06/2025 15:30	10/06/2025 18:01	2	1	9
160	18	10/06/2025 18:01	11/06/2025 20:10	3	2	1
161	19	11/06/2025 20:10	12/06/2025 21:56	4	3	2
162	20	12/06/2025 21:56	13/06/2025 23:20	5	4	3
163	21	13/06/2025 23:20	15/06/2025 00:21	6	5	4
164	22	15/06/2025 00:21	16/06/2025 00:59	7	6	5

Transit of Moon in Nakshatra: 15 Jun to 15 July 2025

SN	NK	Date Entry	Date Exit	X	Y	Z
165	23	16/06/2025 00:59	17/06/2025 01:13	8	7	6
166	24	17/06/2025 01:13	18/06/2025 01:01	9	8	7
167	25	18/06/2025 01:01	19/06/2025 00:22	1	9	8
168	26	19/06/2025 00:22	19/06/2025 23:16	2	1	9
169	27	19/06/2025 23:16	20/06/2025 21:44	3	2	1
170	1	20/06/2025 21:44	21/06/2025 19:49	4	3	2
171	2	21/06/2025 19:49	22/06/2025 17:38	5	4	3
172	3	22/06/2025 17:38	23/06/2025 15:16	6	5	4
173	4	23/06/2025 15:16	24/06/2025 12:53	7	6	5
174	5	24/06/2025 12:53	25/06/2025 10:40	8	7	6
175	6	25/06/2025 10:40	26/06/2025 08:46	9	8	7
176	7	26/06/2025 08:46	27/06/2025 07:21	1	9	8
177	8	27/06/2025 07:21	28/06/2025 06:35	2	1	9
178	9	28/06/2025 06:35	29/06/2025 06:33	3	2	1
179	10	29/06/2025 06:33	30/06/2025 07:20	4	3	2
180	11	30/06/2025 07:20	01/07/2025 08:53	5	4	3
181	12	01/07/2025 08:53	02/07/2025 11:07	6	5	4
182	13	02/07/2025 11:07	03/07/2025 13:50	7	6	5
183	14	03/07/2025 13:50	04/07/2025 16:49	8	7	6
184	15	04/07/2025 16:49	05/07/2025 19:51	9	8	7
185	16	05/07/2025 19:51	06/07/2025 22:41	1	9	8
186	17	06/07/2025 22:41	08/07/2025 01:11	2	1	9
187	18	08/07/2025 01:11	09/07/2025 03:14	3	2	1
188	19	09/07/2025 03:14	10/07/2025 04:49	4	3	2
189	20	10/07/2025 04:49	11/07/2025 05:55	5	4	3
190	21	11/07/2025 05:55	12/07/2025 06:35	6	5	4
191	22	12/07/2025 06:35	13/07/2025 06:52	7	6	5
192	23	13/07/2025 06:52	14/07/2025 06:48	8	7	6
193	24	14/07/2025 06:48	15/07/2025 06:25	9	8	7
194	25	15/07/2025 06:25	16/07/2025 05:46	1	9	8

Transit of Moon in Nakshatra: 16 Jul to 16 Aug 2025

SN	NK	Date Entry	Date Exit	X	Y	Z
195	26	16/07/2025 05:46	17/07/2025 04:50	2	1	9
196	27	17/07/2025 04:50	18/07/2025 03:38	3	2	1
197	1	18/07/2025 03:38	19/07/2025 02:13	4	3	2
198	2	19/07/2025 02:13	20/07/2025 00:37	5	4	3
199	3	20/07/2025 00:37	20/07/2025 22:52	6	5	4
200	4	20/07/2025 22:52	21/07/2025 21:06	7	6	5
201	5	21/07/2025 21:06	22/07/2025 19:24	8	7	6
202	6	22/07/2025 19:24	23/07/2025 17:54	9	8	7
203	7	23/07/2025 17:54	24/07/2025 16:43	1	9	8
204	8	24/07/2025 16:43	25/07/2025 16:00	2	1	9
205	9	25/07/2025 16:00	26/07/2025 15:51	3	2	1
206	10	26/07/2025 15:51	27/07/2025 16:22	4	3	2
207	11	27/07/2025 16:22	28/07/2025 17:35	5	4	3
208	12	28/07/2025 17:35	29/07/2025 19:27	6	5	4
209	13	29/07/2025 19:27	30/07/2025 21:52	7	6	5
210	14	30/07/2025 21:52	01/08/2025 00:41	8	7	6
211	15	01/08/2025 00:41	02/08/2025 03:40	9	8	7
212	16	02/08/2025 03:40	03/08/2025 06:34	1	9	8
213	17	03/08/2025 06:34	04/08/2025 09:12	2	1	9
214	18	04/08/2025 09:12	05/08/2025 11:22	3	2	1
215	19	05/08/2025 11:22	06/08/2025 12:59	4	3	2
216	20	06/08/2025 12:59	07/08/2025 14:01	5	4	3
217	21	07/08/2025 14:01	08/08/2025 14:27	6	5	4
218	22	08/08/2025 14:27	09/08/2025 14:23	7	6	5
219	23	09/08/2025 14:23	10/08/2025 13:52	8	7	6
220	24	10/08/2025 13:52	11/08/2025 12:59	9	8	7
221	25	11/08/2025 12:59	12/08/2025 11:51	1	9	8
222	26	12/08/2025 11:51	13/08/2025 10:32	2	1	9
223	27	13/08/2025 10:32	14/08/2025 09:05	3	2	1
224	1	14/08/2025 09:05	15/08/2025 07:35	4	3	2
225	2	15/08/2025 07:35	16/08/2025 06:05	5	4	3
226	3	16/08/2025 06:05	17/08/2025 04:38	6	5	4

SN	NK	Date Entry	Date Exit	X	Y	Z
		Transit of Moon in Nakshatra: 17 Aug to 16 Sep 2025				
227	4	17/08/2025 04:38	18/08/2025 03:17	7	6	5
228	5	18/08/2025 03:17	19/08/2025 02:05	8	7	6
229	6	19/08/2025 02:05	20/08/2025 01:07	9	8	7
230	7	20/08/2025 01:07	21/08/2025 00:26	1	9	8
231	8	21/08/2025 00:26	22/08/2025 00:08	2	1	9
232	9	22/08/2025 00:08	23/08/2025 00:16	3	2	1
233	10	23/08/2025 00:16	24/08/2025 00:54	4	3	2
234	11	24/08/2025 00:54	25/08/2025 02:05	5	4	3
235	12	25/08/2025 02:05	26/08/2025 03:49	6	5	4
236	13	26/08/2025 03:49	27/08/2025 06:04	7	6	5
237	14	27/08/2025 06:04	28/08/2025 08:43	8	7	6
238	15	28/08/2025 08:43	29/08/2025 11:38	9	8	7
239	16	29/08/2025 11:38	30/08/2025 14:37	1	9	8
240	17	30/08/2025 14:37	31/08/2025 17:26	2	1	9
241	18	31/08/2025 17:26	01/09/2025 19:54	3	2	1
242	19	01/09/2025 19:54	02/09/2025 21:50	4	3	2
243	20	02/09/2025 21:50	03/09/2025 23:08	5	4	3
244	21	03/09/2025 23:08	04/09/2025 23:43	6	5	4
245	22	04/09/2025 23:43	05/09/2025 23:38	7	6	5
246	23	05/09/2025 23:38	06/09/2025 22:55	8	7	6
247	24	06/09/2025 22:55	07/09/2025 21:40	9	8	7
248	25	07/09/2025 21:40	08/09/2025 20:02	1	9	8
249	26	08/09/2025 20:02	09/09/2025 18:06	2	1	9
250	27	09/09/2025 18:06	10/09/2025 16:02	3	2	1
251	1	10/09/2025 16:02	11/09/2025 13:57	4	3	2
252	2	11/09/2025 13:57	12/09/2025 11:58	5	4	3
253	3	12/09/2025 11:58	13/09/2025 10:11	6	5	4
254	4	13/09/2025 10:11	14/09/2025 08:40	7	6	5
255	5	14/09/2025 08:40	15/09/2025 07:31	8	7	6
256	6	15/09/2025 07:31	16/09/2025 06:45	9	8	7
257	7	16/09/2025 06:45	17/09/2025 06:25	1	9	8

Transit of Moon in Nakshatra : 17 Sep to 17 Oct 2025

SN	NK	Date Entry	Date Exit	X	Y	Z
258	8	17/09/2025 06:25	18/09/2025 06:31	2	1	9
259	9	18/09/2025 06:31	19/09/2025 07:05	3	2	1
260	10	19/09/2025 07:05	20/09/2025 08:05	4	3	2
261	11	20/09/2025 08:05	21/09/2025 09:31	5	4	3
262	12	21/09/2025 09:31	22/09/2025 11:23	6	5	4
263	13	22/09/2025 11:23	23/09/2025 13:39	7	6	5
264	14	23/09/2025 13:39	24/09/2025 16:16	8	7	6
265	15	24/09/2025 16:16	25/09/2025 19:08	9	8	7
266	16	25/09/2025 19:08	26/09/2025 22:08	1	9	8
267	17	26/09/2025 22:08	28/09/2025 01:07	2	1	9
268	18	28/09/2025 01:07	29/09/2025 03:54	3	2	1
269	19	29/09/2025 03:54	30/09/2025 06:17	4	3	2
270	20	30/09/2025 06:17	01/10/2025 08:06	5	4	3
271	21	01/10/2025 08:06	02/10/2025 09:12	6	5	4
272	22	02/10/2025 09:12	03/10/2025 09:33	7	6	5
273	23	03/10/2025 09:33	04/10/2025 09:08	8	7	6
274	24	04/10/2025 09:08	05/10/2025 08:00	9	8	7
275	25	05/10/2025 08:00	06/10/2025 06:15	1	9	8
276	26	06/10/2025 06:15	07/10/2025 04:01	2	1	9
277	27	07/10/2025 04:01	08/10/2025 01:27	3	2	1
278	1	08/10/2025 01:27	08/10/2025 22:44	4	3	2
279	2	08/10/2025 22:44	09/10/2025 20:02	5	4	3
280	3	09/10/2025 20:02	10/10/2025 17:30	6	5	4
281	4	10/10/2025 17:30	11/10/2025 15:19	7	6	5
282	5	11/10/2025 15:19	12/10/2025 13:36	8	7	6
283	6	12/10/2025 13:36	13/10/2025 12:26	9	8	7
284	7	13/10/2025 12:26	14/10/2025 11:53	1	9	8
285	8	14/10/2025 11:53	15/10/2025 11:59	2	1	9
286	9	15/10/2025 11:59	16/10/2025 12:41	3	2	1
287	10	16/10/2025 12:41	17/10/2025 13:57	4	3	2
288	11	17/10/2025 13:57	18/10/2025 15:41	5	4	3
289	12	18/10/2025 15:41	19/10/2025 17:49	6	5	4

SN	NK	Date Entry	Date Exit	X	Y	Z
		Transit of Moon in Nakshatra: 18 Oct to 16 Nov 2025				
290	13	19/10/2025 17:49	20/10/2025 20:16	7	6	5
291	14	20/10/2025 20:16	21/10/2025 22:58	8	7	6
292	15	21/10/2025 22:58	23/10/2025 01:51	9	8	7
293	16	23/10/2025 01:51	24/10/2025 04:50	1	9	8
294	17	24/10/2025 04:50	25/10/2025 07:51	2	1	9
295	18	25/10/2025 07:51	26/10/2025 10:46	3	2	1
296	19	26/10/2025 10:46	27/10/2025 13:27	4	3	2
297	20	27/10/2025 13:27	28/10/2025 15:44	5	4	3
298	21	28/10/2025 15:44	29/10/2025 17:29	6	5	4
299	22	29/10/2025 17:29	30/10/2025 18:33	7	6	5
300	23	30/10/2025 18:33	31/10/2025 18:50	8	7	6
301	24	31/10/2025 18:50	01/11/2025 18:20	9	8	7
302	25	01/11/2025 18:20	02/11/2025 17:03	1	9	8
303	26	02/11/2025 17:03	03/11/2025 15:05	2	1	9
304	27	03/11/2025 15:05	04/11/2025 12:34	3	2	1
305	1	04/11/2025 12:34	05/11/2025 09:39	4	3	2
306	2	05/11/2025 09:39	06/11/2025 06:33	5	4	3
307	3	06/11/2025 06:33	07/11/2025 03:27	6	5	4
308	4	07/11/2025 03:27	08/11/2025 00:33	7	6	5
309	5	08/11/2025 00:33	08/11/2025 22:02	8	7	6
310	6	08/11/2025 22:02	09/11/2025 20:04	9	8	7
311	7	09/11/2025 20:04	10/11/2025 18:47	1	9	8
312	8	10/11/2025 18:47	11/11/2025 18:17	2	1	9
313	9	11/11/2025 18:17	12/11/2025 18:34	3	2	1
314	10	12/11/2025 18:34	13/11/2025 19:37	4	3	2
315	11	13/11/2025 19:37	14/11/2025 21:20	5	4	3
316	12	14/11/2025 21:20	15/11/2025 23:34	6	5	4
317	13	15/11/2025 23:34	17/11/2025 02:10	7	6	5

Transit of Moon in Nakshatra: 17 Nov to 15 Dec 2025

SN	NK	Date Entry	Date Exit	X	Y	Z
318	14	17/11/2025 02:10	18/11/2025 05:01	8	7	6
319	15	18/11/2025 05:01	19/11/2025 07:59	9	8	7
320	16	19/11/2025 07:59	20/11/2025 10:58	1	9	8
321	17	20/11/2025 10:58	21/11/2025 13:55	2	1	9
322	18	21/11/2025 13:55	22/11/2025 16:46	3	2	1
323	19	22/11/2025 16:46	23/11/2025 19:27	4	3	2
324	20	23/11/2025 19:27	24/11/2025 21:53	5	4	3
325	21	24/11/2025 21:53	25/11/2025 23:57	6	5	4
326	22	25/11/2025 23:57	27/11/2025 01:32	7	6	5
327	23	27/11/2025 01:32	28/11/2025 02:31	8	7	6
328	24	28/11/2025 02:31	29/11/2025 02:49	9	8	7
329	25	29/11/2025 02:49	30/11/2025 02:22	1	9	8
330	26	30/11/2025 02:22	01/12/2025 01:10	2	1	9
331	27	01/12/2025 01:10	01/12/2025 23:17	3	2	1
332	1	01/12/2025 23:17	02/12/2025 20:51	4	3	2
333	2	02/12/2025 20:51	03/12/2025 17:59	5	4	3
334	3	03/12/2025 17:59	04/12/2025 14:53	6	5	4
335	4	04/12/2025 14:53	05/12/2025 11:45	7	6	5
336	5	05/12/2025 11:45	06/12/2025 08:48	8	7	6
337	6	06/12/2025 08:48	07/12/2025 06:13	9	8	7
338	7	07/12/2025 06:13	08/12/2025 04:11	1	9	8
339	8	08/12/2025 04:11	09/12/2025 02:52	2	1	9
340	9	09/12/2025 02:52	10/12/2025 02:22	3	2	1
341	10	10/12/2025 02:22	11/12/2025 02:43	4	3	2
342	11	11/12/2025 02:43	12/12/2025 03:55	5	4	3
343	12	12/12/2025 03:55	13/12/2025 05:49	6	5	4
344	13	13/12/2025 05:49	14/12/2025 08:18	7	6	5
345	14	14/12/2025 08:18	15/12/2025 11:08	8	7	6
346	15	15/12/2025 11:08	16/12/2025 14:09	9	8	7

Transit of Moon in Nakshatra: 16 Dec to 31 Dec 2025

SN	NK	Date Entry	Date Exit	X	Y	Z
347	16	16/12/2025 14:09	17/12/2025 17:11	1	9	8
348	17	17/12/2025 17:11	18/12/2025 20:06	2	1	9
349	18	18/12/2025 20:06	19/12/2025 22:50	3	2	1
350	19	19/12/2025 22:50	21/12/2025 01:21	4	3	2
351	20	21/12/2025 01:21	22/12/2025 03:35	5	4	3
352	21	22/12/2025 03:35	23/12/2025 05:32	6	5	4
353	22	23/12/2025 05:32	24/12/2025 07:07	7	6	5
354	23	24/12/2025 07:07	25/12/2025 08:18	8	7	6
355	24	25/12/2025 08:18	26/12/2025 09:00	9	8	7
356	25	26/12/2025 09:00	27/12/2025 09:09	1	9	8
357	26	27/12/2025 09:09	28/12/2025 08:42	2	1	9
358	27	28/12/2025 08:42	29/12/2025 07:40	3	2	1
359	1	29/12/2025 07:40	30/12/2025 06:03	4	3	2
360	2	30/12/2025 06:03	31/12/2025 03:57	5	4	3
361	3	31/12/2025 03:57		6	5	4

SCORPIO SIGN AS WHOLE

Scorpio, the eighth zodiac sign, is ruled by the planet Mars and is an extremely powerful sign, known for its potential for both good and evil. Its symbol is Scorpio. This sign signifies affection and attachment. Scorpios are often referred to as the detectives of the zodiac. As per the Sun astrology, people born during the period 23 Oct to 22 Nov fall under the Scorpio sign.

The alphabets that come under this sign are To, Tho, Na, Nau, Ni, Nee, Nu, Noo, Ne, Nay, No, Nau, Ya, Yi, Yee, Yu, Yoo.

Water is the associated element for Scorpio, and although their emotions are as deep as other Water signs, Scorpios tend to keep their feelings repressed and hidden. This secretive and intense nature contributes to their ability to see through situations and individuals. Scorpios may become vindictive if they feel crossed, but they usually return to their determined and loyal ways once they regain composure.

Scorpios are ruled by Mars and Ketu (Pluto). Mars, the God of War, is the first ruler of Scorpio, and when combined with Ketu, known as the God of the Underworld, it brings intense energy to those born under this sign. Due to the influence of Mars, natives may be passionate, intense and assertive. In the Aries, the lower Mars rules where the person is more offensive but in the case of Scorpio, the upper Mars rules make the person have more resistance to any changes. Scorpios are motivated, penetrating, and highly attuned to the vibrations of others. They can be fearless, often rebounding from setbacks with regenerative powers, displaying their stubborn and determined nature. Ketu is associated with spiritual pursuits, detachment, and karmic influences. In Scorpio, this may add depth to the individual's spiritual interests and journey.

In astrology charts, when Scorpio influences a house or planet, it brings about characteristics such as secrecy, coercion, deep emotions and desires, jealousy, intense conflicts, possessiveness, forced changes, sometimes a fatalistic attitude, and areas where meanness may prevail.

This zodiac sign is linked to Brahmins and is said to reside in holes, having its connection to hidden or mysterious aspects. Scorpio is aligned with the North direction and is strong during the daytime. The color associated with Scorpio is reddish-brown. Due to their affiliation with both water and land, they have a connection to dual elements and environments indicating adaptability and versatility. Scorpio is shishodaya, "head-first", indicating a focused, determined, and goal-oriented approach to life. Scorpio is associated with the rago-guna or rajas. It is associated with the water element (Jal Tatva), which signifies emotional depth, intuition, and fluidity in character.

Scorpio native possesses a well-proportioned body, with long hands and an above-average stature. They have a hairy physique, indicating a certain ruggedness or passion. Their facial features include a broad face with a commanding appearance, contributing to an overall good personality.

The symbol, Scorpion reflects their determination, control, and ability to regenerate, much like the literal Scorpion that can grow a new tail. The Individuals born under this sign are known for their serious and probing nature. Scorpios are highly focused on learning about others and are not interested in superficial conversations. They are adept investigators with an immeasurable curiosity, always seeking the truth and delving into the depths of any matter.

Scorpions are resourceful, passionate, stubborn, brave and a true friend until the end. They appreciate the truth, longtime friends and have fun teasing those they are comfortable with. The sign that represents Scorpios typifies them well. Scorpions aren't necessarily aggressive until they are provoked and, even then, they would rather be contemplative as opposed to fight. They are excellent keepers of secrets and feel emotions much more intensely than any other sign. Because of this, they can help people with their problems and can get to the root of any issue.

Scorpios possess a strong willpower and intense emotional drive, often reflected in their robust sex drive. They approach everything with intensity and completeness, displaying no fear of death. Due to their emotional intensity, Scorpios must maintain high integrity to avoid undesirable behaviors like violence, jealousy, hatred, or possessiveness.

Workaholic tendencies are common among Scorpios, who not only drive themselves hard but also expect the same from others. They despise weakness in themselves and others, often providing help but expecting recipients to become self-sufficient quickly. Scorpios are known for their secrecy and can be ruthless enemies or competitors.

Typical Scorpio traits include being vindictive, sarcastic, heroic, forceful, cynical, secretive, determined, and suspicious. Their interests often revolve around sex, unraveling mysteries, controlling others' money, and wielding unseen power.

Scorpios never forget it, once they've been wronged. They can also be pessimistic and see threats when there aren't any. That makes them suspicious, paranoid and stubborn without any real cause.

On the upside, Scorpios have self-control in almost every other area of their lives. Likewise, they expect the same from others. They are protective and disciplined. They are very giving and, again, expect the same in return.

Scorpios love competition, thriving in both work and play. They are drawn to extreme sports and challenges that test their mettle. The colors associated with Scorpio are powerful red and serious black. In love, Scorpios can be caring and devoted, but their passionate and intense nature may lead to possessiveness. Their strength lies in determination, passion, and motivation, making them a powerhouse in various aspects of life.

On a deeper level, Scorpios are described as enigmatic and capable of significant metamorphosis and renewal. They are considered a Plutonian power force, favoring stability while embracing intense emotions. A fixed nature makes Scorpios prone to extremes, and maintaining inner security helps balance their intense emotions and possessive tendencies. Overall, Scorpios are known for their strength, determination, and profound understanding of life and relationships.

Scorpio individuals have a strong determination to overcome obstacles and move forward in the pursuit of their goals.

This zodiac sign is associated with a fertile imagination and sharp intelligence. Despite being emotional, Scorpio natives have a remarkable intuitive power. They possess self-assertion, courage, resolution, independence, and forcefulness. They express a keen interest in occult sciences and spiritual experiments.

Scorpio individuals have a harsh tongue. They tend to be revengeful and vindictive, showing a propensity for criticism as a means of establishing their superiority.

The domestic life of a Scorpio individual is deemed to be happy only if every family member is submissive to them. These individuals tend to engage in relations with multiple partners.

REMEDIES FOR SCORPIO

Mars is the ruling planet for Scorpio. Mars rules the Lagna and the sixth house in the Scorpio chart. The sixth house is the house of debt, disease and enemies, A strong Mars can provide good health, victory over enemies, freedom from debts, success in competitions, happiness from life partner and siblings, success in the profession, and all luxuries in life. In certain cases, the position of Mars in a person's horoscope chart can have negative effects due to its association with malefic plates, unfavorable placement or weak strength. In such situations, it is important to consider remedies to mitigate the negative impacts of Mars. These remedies are beneficial in reducing the adverse effects. You can choose one of the remedies or combine two or three of them to lessen Mars's wrath when it is malefic in your chart.

Remedies for Mars

A strong Mars in the Scorpio chart has the potential to bestow good health, success in ventures, good relations with siblings, good physical stamina, inheritance, and gains from undisclosed sources. However, if you encounter issues related to finances, professional issues, frequent job changes, problems in communication or social relationships, problems with or with brothers, and in vitality, low energy levels, high Blood pressure, anger outbursts, problems with children or at professional front, it signifies an afflicted and inauspicious Mars in your chart. Even if they find that their desires are not fulfilled, they should check Mars. To alleviate this situation, several measures can be taken.

Mars is the planet of energy and Vitality and it gets its energy from the Sun. You should wake up early morning and do exercise. Your life routine should be active to keep Mars's energies drained out positively. If Mars is not positioned in the sixth, eighth, or twelfth house, wearing a red coral or its substitute on the ring finger of the right hand is advisable. However, Scorpio should avoid wearing Red Coral as it will activate the sixth house also. Wearing a saffron color thread on the right wrist will be an effective remedy. Do not be egoistic and arrogant with others. Standing with those who need help can also serve as an effective remedy. Mars is ruled by Lord Hanuman who has devoted himself selflessly to Lord Rama. Those having professional issues should consider devoting their energies to the cause of the organization and hence their seniors. They will continue to have problems in their profession if they have a different agenda from their boss.

Remedies for Sun

Sun is the lord of the Leo sign and the tenth house in the Scorpio chart. It rules over the house of profession for Scorpio. An auspicious Sun bestows a range of positive attributes upon the individual. This includes a strong body constitution, a royal lifestyle, artistic and creative talents, good finances and support of family control over enemies, free from disease and debt, and support from higher-ups. The influence of the Sun contributes to the native's overall charm and harmonious interactions with family members. A strong Sun in the chart of Scorpio ensures that a person reaches to pinnacles of his profession.

If the Sun is afflicted, weak or inauspicious, then the native is devoid of good attributes as we discussed. Reciting of Surya Mantra 7000 times will be quite a helpful remedy.

If the Sun is not posted in the eighth or twelfth house, then the native should wear a Ruby ring or necklace to give it strength.

Remedies for Moon

Moon is the ruling planet for the Cancer Sign and the ninth house in the Scorpio chart. It controls Scorpio's Sluck, higher education, spirituality, and foreign travels. In astrology, the Moon represents emotions, intuition, the subconscious mind, and the feminine principle. In case you are having problems in these aspects and overall obstacles in life, apart from the planet, which is causing obstacles, you need to do the remedy for the Moon to strengthen it. If Moon is strong, then despite resistance in life, you will get success. The position of the Moon in your birth chart is believed to influence your emotional responses, instincts, and overall well-being. I generally check the condition and health of the mother, emotional strength of individuals, health of individual and life path to know the condition of Moon apart from his birth chart. Any problems there need to be addressed by doing remedy for Moon. In Vedic astrology, the Moon has been given the highest importance over Lagna and Sun Sign. So let us find out what remedies can be done for the afflicted moon or to strengthen the Moon.

White Pearl is the gemstone associated with the Moon in astrology. Wearing a white pearl is believed to enhance the positive qualities of the Moon and promote emotional balance. Silver is the metal associated with the Moon. In the Hindu system, any newborn child having longevity issues, cough and cold, and slow mental progress is made to wear a pendant with a round silver piece. Even otherwise, children are made to wear bracelets made of silver for good health.

Those who can afford to use silver cutlery for children. Even for consumption, silver foil is used to put over sweets and even in Milk. I find it as most effective means to strengthen the Moon. If the Moon or Mind is strong, the person can overcome any resistance in life.

Monday is considered the day of the Moon and fasting on Mondays is believed to appease the Moon and strengthen its positive influence. Some people fast by consuming only liquids or specific types of food on Mondays.

Chanting specific mantras associated with the Moon can be a remedy. The most common mantra is the "Chandra Mantra" or "Moon Mantra" - "Om Som Somaya Namaha." Regular chanting is believed to bring peace and harmony.

Lord Shiva holds the key to all longevity and marriage issues. Maha Mritunjay Mantra is found to be the best mantra for health and longevity issues. Worship Lord Shiva every day. Offer milk to the Shivling while chanting the Shiv Chalisa or the Om Namah Shivaya mantra 108 times.

Engaging in rituals or ceremonies dedicated to the Moon, especially on Full Moon days, is thought to enhance the positive energy of the Moon. Practices such as meditation, prayer, or simply spending time in quiet reflection can be beneficial. Meditating under the moonlight is strongly advised for strengthening a weak Moon.

Making charitable donations, especially on Mondays, is believed to bring positive lunar energy. Donating white clothes to the poor and the needy can also prove to be helpful.

In astrology, the Moon is often associated with the fourth house, which represents home, family, and emotional security. Strengthening your connection with these areas of life through positive actions and intentions can help balance lunar energies. You should always honor your mother and other elders at home.

Remedies for Mercury

Mercury rules Gemini and Virgo signs. It also rules the eighth and eleventh houses of the chart. The eighth house is the house of obstacles, obstructions, losses, delays and even inheritance. The eleventh house is associated with elder siblings, social networks, gains and fulfillment of desires. Interestingly, Mercury is controlling the obstacles and gains both in the Scorpio chart.

It represents wisdom, intelligence, and the potential for financial success, whether through ethical or unethical means. If Mercury is weak, natives will have certain health and professional issues. Firstly, we need to understand the signification of Mercury as it should not happen that you are doing remedy of the Planet which is not related to the problem. I will cover the remedies of Mercury here in detail and other planets in summarised form.

Mercury is the planet of communication. In the human body, communication is through the nerves which transmit data from the brain to body muscles and vice versa. It signifies our nervous system, reflexes which are controlled by nerves at the internal level. Mercury has a direct impact on the grey matter and CNS (central nervous system) of our head.

At the exterior end, the mouth, tongue, vocal cord, and lungs as they provide air to the lungs for communication. For communication, hearing and sight provide primary inputs. Hands and arms are means to communicate through nonverbal communication. Speech is the most effective means of communication and Mercury rules speech. It rules over the mouth, tongue, eyesight, and ears as they also mean communication.

Mercury rules over the skin as the skin is the sense organ. All skin-related diseases are due to the malefic effect of Mercury. Besides skin, Mercury has direct control over the maturation and action of white blood cells or leucocytes in our body. Mercury, while in affliction may cause an imbalance in the production of leucocytes (white blood cells) which as a result may cause leukoderma (white disease) in the skin and even cause leukemia (abnormal high count of leucocytes) which is commonly known as blood cancer.

Mercury, being the natural ruler of the sixth house, rules over the digestive fire. The natural second house or Venus signifies the taste of food or intake of food whereas the sixth house is the appetite and dictates when to stop eating or when to eat, as it controls hunger, appetite, and digestion. Mercury also rules Biles, wind, phlegm, anus, and thighs.

A favorable placement of Mercury in a person's birth chart is believed to contribute to academic success. It may indicate a natural aptitude for learning, good memory retention, and the ability to grasp complex concepts quickly. It indicates mental dexterity which means how fast one can frame and express the thought process in different mediums or languages.

In matters of relations, Mercury represents a person's sister, sister-in-law or even widow elder ladies in the family. In case, Mercury is afflicted native will have a problem in all the significations as discussed above, then he should do the remedies for Mercury as being discussed now. You can choose one of the remedies or combine two or three of them to lessen Mercury's wrath when it is malefic in your chart.

Green Emerald is the gemstone to strengthens Mercury and gives auspicious results. Its results are more prevalent in the period, of Dasha and Antardasha, of Mercury. It should be worn only if Mercury is not afflicted or not ruling planet for the 6th, 8th or 12th house of the chart. Green Emerald should be worn in a ring with either gold or silver on the little finger of the right hand for males and left hand for females, specifically on Wednesdays. The weight of the Emerald should be at least 4 carats and free from flaws and defects. It can also be worn in a pendant. Small rituals should be performed before wearing the gemstone emerald. Dip the ring either in the holy water (water from holy rivers or sacred ponds) or cow milk early in the morning on Wednesday of the bright fortnight (Shukla Paksha) and perform a Puja with the mantra "Om Bhum Budhay Namah" 108 times. It may help to overcome various obstacles such as mental disorders, loss of confidence, communication difficulties, and educational challenges. All gemstones should be tested before wearing.

Budh Yantra is another effective means to remove the ill effects of Budha or Mercury. One can wear a Budh Yantra made of silver or copper as a pendant. This Yantra can also be kept in the Puja place at home after proper Puja (Pran Pratistha).

Another remedy associated with Mercury is the four Mukhi Rudraksha bead, which is linked to Lord Brahma, the divine embodiment of wisdom and knowledge, who is also considered the ruler of Mercury. Wearing this Rudraksha bead can help harness the positive energies associated with Mercury and promote mental clarity and intellectual growth.

Fasting or observing a vrat (religious fast) for Mercury or Budh can be done to appease the planet and mitigate any malefic effects. The planet Mercury is associated with Lord Budha, who is considered a divine representation and is believed to be a reincarnation of Lord

Krishna or Lord Vishnu. To seek blessings and counteract the negative influences of Mercury, devotees worship Lord Vishnu or Lord Krishna on Wednesdays and observe a fast dedicated to them.

To appease Mercury, one can offer gold, green cloth, green vegetables, and green-colored bangles, writing materials to poor students, as these are considered appealing to the planet. Other items that can be donated for Mercury include ivory, sugar, black gram, camphor, and turpentine oil. Helping poor students can also bring positive results. It is recommended to perform these charitable acts on Wednesdays, within two hours before sunset.

Mercury's association with mental faculties and communication gives it a natural inclination and ability to engage in the repetitive chanting of mantras. This quality makes it beneficial for spiritual practices and Vedic remedies. These practices aim to address and alleviate obstructions or afflictions in specific areas of one's life. Typically, they involve dedicating a few minutes or hours every day for a period of 40 days or even a year to repetitively recite a specific mantra. In some cases, the mantra may need to be repeated 100,000 times. As one embarks on this journey, the mantra gradually starts to manifest its effects, which may occasionally involve confronting challenging experiences as personal limitations and dysfunctions are addressed.

Chanting the Beeja Mantra of Budha (Mercury) can be done a specific number of times based on the placement of Mercury in one's horoscope chart. One can chant the Budh Beeja mantra 108 times or its multiples in one sitting. Rituals associated with the worship of Mercury include honoring Lord Vishnu and Lord Brahma and reciting the "Sahasranama Stotra."

Furthermore, chanting the Budha Mantra or Stotra 17,000 times is believed to be beneficial. This should be done in a well-planned manner over 40 days, with the prescribed timing of two hours after sunrise on Wednesdays. It is important to ensure physical and mental cleanliness and purity before chanting this mantra. Here are some mantras associated with Budh:

Budha Mantra: "Om Bhum Bhudaaya namah"

Budha Beej Mantra: "Om bhraam bhreem bhroum saha budhaaya namaha"

Budha Gayatri Mantra: "Om Gajadhwajaaya Vidmahae Sukha Hastaaya Dheemahi Tanno Budha Prachodayaat"

Budha Navagraha Mantra: "Priyam gukalikaashyaamam Rupenaam prathimam Budham Saumyam Saumya gunorpetham tham Budham pranamaamyaham"

To please the deity of Mercury, there are several practices and beliefs, such as:

Green is considered the favorite color of Mercury, representing vegetation on Earth. Carrying a green handkerchief is believed to bring positive energies associated with Mercury.

Planting a banana tree on Wednesdays in the surrounding environment is considered auspicious for Mercury. The Banana tree is associated with Jupiter and those who have Jupiter as their Badhak as Dual signs Gemini, Virgo, Sagittarius or Pisces will gain more from this. This stabilizes the energies of Jupiter which are creating hurdles by the gesture of surrender.

Walking barefoot on grass is thought to enhance the connection with Mercury's energies. This is due to the activation of nerves through the feet by acupressure.

Tulsi, also known as holy basil, holds great significance in the

Hindu belief system and is deeply associated with Lord Krishna, as it is believed that Radha transformed into a Tulsi plant. Nurturing a Tulsi plant and tending to it daily, except on Sundays, is considered an act of expressing gratitude to Lord Krishna. Additionally, consuming Tulsi leaves, known for their medicinal properties, is believed to fortify the influence of Mercury.

Offering green grass to cows is regarded as a significant remedy for mitigating the effects of a malefic Mercury. Cows hold a profound association with Lord Krishna. It is recommended to feed cows an amount of grass equivalent to one's body weight, preferably on Wednesdays. Administering this remedy for four consecutive Wednesdays is believed to be particularly effective in counteracting the malefic influence of Mercury. It is important to note that this remedy is more suitable for addressing the malefic aspect of Mercury rather than its weakness.

If a person has a weak mind, that is, a weak Mercury, they can improve it through meditation and the use of Ayurvedic medicines such as Brahmi and Shankhapushpi. These herbs have an association with the Lord Brahma and Lord Vishnu.

Worshipping Mata Durga and recitation of Durga Saptashati is also a very effective remedy.

Offering a sweet dish made of milk to Lord Brahma, who is associated with Mercury, is considered auspicious and beneficial. It is worth noting that Lord Brahma is not widely worshipped in the Hindu system, and there is only one temple dedicated to him in Pushkar, Rajasthan. Lord Brahma bestowed the name Budha upon Mercury due to its intelligence and intellect. Pleasing Lord Brahma is believed to reduce the adverse effects of Mercury and bring about positive outcomes.

Engaging in businesses related to items such as silver, gold, bronze, elephant tooth, ready-made garments, oil, fruits, poultry, and vegetables is believed to bring favorable results associated with Mercury.

According to Lal Kitab, fixing four bronze nails in the four corners of a bed or house is believed to ward off negative energies and promote harmony. Lal Kitab suggests that piercing the nose can be beneficial. Cleaning teeth with alum and worshipping unmarried girls are also recommended remedies to alleviate troubles caused by malefic Mercury. Showing respect and kindness towards elders, aunts, family members, sisters, cousins, and even eunuchs is advised to please the deity associated with Mercury. Additionally, showing respect to eunuchs is also considered a remedy for Mercury. Piercing of ears is one of the practices that has been used for centuries in the Hindu system and is believed to give good results.

Those students who find difficulty in concentration while studying are recommended to keep a peacock feather in their study room. The bird that can be associated with Mercury is Parrot. This may be due to its green color or its ability to talk like humans. Keeping a parrot or feeding a parrot is also a good remedy in this regard.

Remedies for Jupiter

For Scorpio, Jupiter is the lord of the second and fifth houses of the chart. The second house rules over speech, communication, food, family and finances whereas the ninth house signifies luck, religion, higher education, law, spirituality, and long travels. The fifth house is associated with education, children, love relationships, enjoyment, speculations and creativity. If there are issues related to marriage, happiness from family, purchasing a house or property, business, or projection in public, then natives should remedy for Jupiter.

I would recommend that a cotton thread dipped in yellow turmeric be wrapped around a Peepal tree in a temple on Thursday. For any other Jupiter-related issues, planting a Peepal tree on Thursday is found to be a very effective remedy for Jupiter. Apart from this, recite the mantras for Jupiter. To harness its maximum benefits, practitioners are encouraged to recite this mantra a total of 19,000 times. As an offering of devotion, present fresh yellow flowers and traditional yellow sweets to Guru Brihaspati. These offerings symbolize your reverence and commitment to the practice. To keep track of your repetitions, employ a Tulsi mala, a sacred rosary made from holy basil beads. It is crucial to complete the full 19,000 repetitions, and the Tulsi mala assists in this task. Thursday, associated with Guru Brihaspati, is the most propitious day to undertake this mantra-chanting practice. The powerful mantras of Jupiter are as under: -

|| **Om Gram Grim Groom Sah Guruvey Namah** ||

|| **Devaanaanca rishinaanca gurum kaancana sannibham**

Buddhi bhutam trilokesham tam namaami brihaaspatim

Om gurave namah ||

|| **Om Suraachaarya Vidmahe, Surasreshtaya Dhimahi, Tanno**
Guruh Prachodayat ||

Remedies for Venus

Venus is the lord of the seventh and twelfth houses in the Scorpio chart. The seventh house signifies married life, marriage, and sex organs.

It also signifies your business partner, and how the world perceives you. The twelfth house is the house of transformation, expenditure, losses, detachment and attachment.

An auspicious Venus bestows a range of positive attributes upon the individual. This includes good health, artistic and creative talents, physical beauty, intelligence, diplomatic skills, affectionate demeanour, gentleness, gracefulness, and reliability. The influence of Venus contributes to the native's overall charm and harmonious interactions with others. If Venus is afflicted, weak or inauspicious, then native is devoid of good attributes as we discussed. If Venus is not posted in the sixth, eighth or twelfth house, then the native should wear a Diamond in a ring or necklace to give it strength. Those having a low sexual urge or lesser sperm and not becoming parents may consume "Heera Bhasam", an Ayurvedic medicine to increase sexual urge or increase sperm count. This is generally available in all Ayurvedic stores. Advice from any Ayurvedic Doctor can be taken in this regard. The native should wear good dresses, perfume, jewellery and good quality stuff in their life. Worship of Maa Durga or keeping fast on Fridays will give good results.

Please remember that remedies are meant to address manageable planetary challenges. If any planet has more than three afflictions, it's considered incurable or Pakka Karmas where remedies might not be effective. In such cases, individuals have to face the consequences. We must have faith in God and ourselves and keep doing our deeds. By continuing to perform your actions with dedication, everything will eventually fall into its rightful place.

Remedies for Saturn

Saturn rules over Capricorn and Aquarius signs and also rules the third and fourth houses of the Scorpio chart. The third house rules over communications and siblings whereas the fourth house signifies happiness from family, luxuries and comfort at home, state of your mother, emotions, feelings and even heart.

A strong Saturn in the Scorpio chart has the potential for longevity, a happy family life, good sleep, enjoyment and comfort at home, house, land, success in ventures, success, robust health. However, if you encounter issues related to knees, legs, Vata imbalances, hair loss, or frequent turnover of servants or employees, it signifies an afflicted and inauspicious Saturn. Saturn calls for discipline, hard work, and patience to harness its positive influences and mitigate its challenging effects.

I will mention a few remedies for Saturn as per Vedic astrology and Lal Kitab which can be performed to obtain auspicious results of Saturn.

According to Vedic Astrology, donation is considered the most effective way to alleviate the malefic effects of a planet. This practice not only helps counteract negative influences but also allows individuals to perform virtuous deeds to atone for their sins. However, this donation should be carried out with sincerity, and faith, and without expecting anything in return. Donations are ideally given to a deserving and suitable person.

To mitigate the adverse effects of Saturn, donations related to this planet should be made on a Saturday, particularly during Saturn Hora and Saturn's Nakshatra (Pushya, Anuradha, Uttara Bhadrapada) in the evening. Items such as Black Lentil (Sabut Urad), Iron, Mustard Oil, Sesame Seeds, Male Buffalo and Black Clothes are suggested for donation as part of Saturn remedies.

If Saturn is not placed in the eighth or twelfth house of the chart, wearing of Blue Sapphire gemstone on the middle finger is the most effective remedy. In case you find Blue Sapphire, the cost is beyond your means, may use any substitute of Blue Sapphire.

Wearing of ring made of a black horseshoe or the nail of the sea boat on your middle finger is considered an effective remedy for Saturn.

To appease and to receive blessings of Planet Saturn you should recite Shani Beej Mantra: -

"Aum Praam Preem Proum Sah Shanaishcharaye Namah !"

This mantra should be chanted four cycles of 23000 times means 92000 times. This can be done in 40 days.

Yantras are special designs that go along with mantras to make them more effective. They're useful when you can't say the mantra out loud, when you need a symbol for a deity, or when buying gemstones is too expensive. Yantras are usually drawn on a type of parchment called Bhojpatra and worn as a lucky charm on the body. If you can't make one, you can also engrave the design on a small pendant. Each of the Nine planets has its specific yantra, and together they're called the Navgrah yantra. Shani Yantra activates number 6.

12	7	14
13	11	9
8	15	10

Other Remedies

Perform mopping and cleaning at the entrance or main passage of a religious place. This is believed to bring positive energy and spiritual purification. It shows that you are devoting yourself to the mankind and shedding your ego. In Sikhism, there is concept of shoe service where people do the service as handling and cleaning of shoes of devotees coming to shrines. Even distributing food to devotees at the shrine is a good remedy. Feed ants with wheat flour as a form of charity.

Looking at the shadow of your face in mustard oil and then draining that oil to an isolated tree removes negativity. This act, known as Chaya Patra Daan, is thought to promote positive karma and goodwill. To increase the auspiciousness of Saturn, a person should feed the birds seven mixed grains or pulses on Saturdays.

Help the needy, less fortunate and differently abled individuals in your community. Ensure that those around you, including associates, servants, and laborers, are content and happy. Remain humble and shed your ego.

Avoid black-colored clothing as a part of your regular attire. Avoid the consumption of liquor, fish, eggs, or non-vegetarian foods. Refrain from drinking milk at night. Consume black grams on Saturday and high protein diets regularly. You may pour black Urad seeds into the flowing water. Offering a mustard oil-smeared Roti to a dog or a crow.\ is also a good remedy. You should avoid buying rubber or iron-related items on Saturdays. You should go for regular walks.

Please note that these recommendations are general and based on astrological beliefs. For personalised remedies, it is recommended that you should consult an astrologer.

****

Please remember that astrological remedies are based on belief systems, religion and faith. If you are interested in personalised astrological remedies, you are most welcome to contact us at astrogauatmdk@gmail.com.

Wishing you another wonderful year in 2025

AFTERWORD

Astrology is an enchanting subject that holds the secrets of our life's purpose. If we can understand even a part of it, we are considered fortunate. Each planet influences different aspects of human life, and some effects may go beyond our logical understanding. Learning more often makes us realize how much there is to explore, like taking a spoonful of water from an ocean of knowledge.

In this book, we have attempted to provide general predictions for this zodiac sign for the year 2025. We suggest taking these predictions as warnings to prepare yourself accordingly. We may not cover everything, as there is no limit to this field. Predicting events is a complex process because of the intricate connections between planets, signs, houses, Nakshatras, and their Padas. We rely on God's blessings and use our experience and knowledge to make predictions. However, the results may vary for each person depending on their natal chart, life phase, age, background, and location.

In the predictions for 2024, I have found a large number of events happened as predicted at different places. It reinforced our belief in the science of astrology. I encourage readers to share feedback on the insights discussed in this book so that we can all learn from each other's experiences. Together, we can discover more about the fascinating world of astrology and its impact on our lives.

Please remember wheel of time is always moving. Transit of planet in one Sign or another will continue. In an earthquake, weak houses get damaged. Houses having strong foundations and structures continue to stand tall even after a strong earthquake. Similarly, those who have strong motivation, character, and relationships will stand past any transit with minor vibrations. Do not worry much about the transit but make yourself strong with hard work, dedication, and good deeds.

God Bless You

PREVIOUS PREDICTIONS THAT BECOME TRUE

In the Annual Horoscope 2024 series, I have made some predictions that have proved true. Regarding Earthquakes, during Saturn Mars, conjunction from 15 Mar to 23 Apr 2024 May 2025 - An earthquake of magnitude 7.4 occurred on 02 Apr 2024 16 km S of Hualien City event in Taiwan. Predictions about intense rains, forest fires, train accidents in my Annual Horoscope 2024 as per timelines have been turned true.

Allegation over political parties and the future of AAP and Kejriwal – A lot of politicians have been maligned and Arvind Kejriwal, President of AAP was arrested and has been in jail with no hope of release. AAP party is likely to be declared as a beneficiary of corruption and may be banned. Fire incidents and accidents in May – June 2024, many such incidents have happened.

Regarding BJP victory in General Elections 2024- Despite the BJP slogan "400 Paar", my prediction regarding BJP is to work hard to form a government and take the support of others to prove the majority. BJP could get only 241 seats against the requirement of 272 so it will be forced to take the support of some parties to form government. We find that the BJP has formed the government but with the support of other parties. The parliament sessions are found to be quite noisy.

Ukraine-Russia issues remain unresolved. Ghaza, Palestine, and rising support for Palestine, the world is witnessing increased support regarding that. Iran is also getting involved and this turn may result in war on a larger scale by Mar 2025.

Conversions are on the rise and the world is looking for this rise in a serious manner. Similarly, there is quite an unrest in France, the UK, the US, Spain, Greece, the Netherlands, etc over the elections. Left-wing and Right-wing parties of these countries have the major agenda of migrant issues. Donald Trump is fighting the election on the same issues.

Stock markets have risen all over the world markets has been recorded and markets are at their peak. They will continue to hold good till Oct 2025 with some correction.

UK PM has been replaced by the left wing. US ex-President Donald Trump has gone through an assassination attempt and in the forthcoming elections, he is likely to be elected as next President. Unrest in some countries as predicted, Bangla Desh PM is on the run after civil unrest.

As discussed, the BJP government has come under pressure from opposition parties and started the Unified Pension Scheme which is rolling back to the Old Pension scheme. Even in Maharashtra, it has gone for lucrative freebies such as the Ladli Behan scheme which it is giving rs 1500 per month to ladies. However, economic blunders still have been forced to be announced.

PM Sh Modi visited Ukraine and he may be able to mediate to find a solution to Russia and Ukraine's problem. Monkeypox virus is becoming an issue and the same has been mentioned in our 2024 Annual Horoscope, though the name of the virus was not there.

TRANSIT OF PLANETS IN 2025

S. No	Planet	Event	Sign	Entry Date	Exit Date
1	Saturn	enters	Aquarius	18-06-2023	29-03-2025
2	Rahu	enters	Pisces	30-10-2023	18-05-2025
3	Ketu	enters	Virgo	30-10-2023	18-05-2025
4	Jupiter	Retrograde in	Taurus	09-10-2024	04-02-2025
5	Mars	enters	Cancer	20-10-2024	21-01-2025
6	Mercury	enters	Scorpio	29-10-2024	04-01-2025
7	Saturn	Direct in	Aquarius	15-11-2024	13-07-2025
8	Mars	Retrograde in	Cancer	07-12-2024	
9	Venus	enters	Aquarius	28-12-2024	28-01-2025
10	Mercury	enters	Sagittarius	04-01-2025	24-01-2025
11	Sun	enters	Capricorn	14-01-2025	12-02-2025
12	Mars	enters	Gemini	21-01-2025	03-04-2025
13	Mercury	enters	Capricorn	24-01-2025	11-02-2025
14	Venus	enters	Pisces	28-01-2025	31-05-2025
15	Jupiter	Direct in	Taurus	04-02-2025	11-11-2025
16	Mercury	enters	Aquarius	11-02-2025	27-02-2025
17	Sun	enters	Aquarius	12-02-2025	14-03-2025
18	Mars	Direct in	Gemini	24-02-2025	
19	Mercury	enters	Pisces	27-02-2025	07-05-2025
20	Venus	Retrograde in	Pisces	02-03-2025	
21	Śun	enters	Pisces	14-03-2025	14-04-2025
22	Mercury	Retrograde in	Pisces	15-03-2025	
23	Saturn	enters	Pisces	29-03-2025	03-06-2027
24	Mars	enters	Cancer	03-04-2025	07-06-2025

| 25 | Mercury | Direct in | Pisces | 07-04-2025 | |

26	Venus	Direct in	Pisces	13-04-2025	
27	Sun	enters	Aries	14-04-2025	15-05-2025
28	Mercury	enters	Aries	07-05-2025	23-05-2025
29	Jupiter	enters	Gemini	14-05-2025	18-10-2025
30	Sun	enters	Taurus	15-05-2025	15-06-2025
31	Rahu	enters	Aquarius	18-05-2025	05-12-2026
32	Mercury	enters	Taurus	23-05-2025	06-06-2025
33	Venus	enters	Aries	31-05-2025	29-06-2025
34	Mercury	enters	Gemini	06-06-2025	22-06-2025
35	Mars	enters	Leo	07-06-2025	28-07-2025
36	Sun	enters	Gemini	15-06-2025	16-07-2025
37	Mercury	enters	Cancer	22-06-2025	30-08-2025
38	Venus	enters	Taurus	29-06-2025	26-07-2025
39	Saturn	Retrograde in	Pisces	13-07-2025	28-11-2025
40	Sun	enters	Cancer	16-07-2025	17-08-2025
41	Mercury	Retrograde in	Cancer	18-07-2025	
42	Venus	enters	Gemini	26-07-2025	21-08-2025
43	Mars	enters	Virgo	28-07-2025	13-09-2025
44	Mercury	Direct in	Cancer	11-08-2025	
45	Sun	enters	Leo	17-08-2025	17-09-2025
46	Venus	enters	Cancer	21-08-2025	15-09-2025
47	Mercury	enters	Leo	30-08-2025	15-09-2025
48	Mars	enters	Libra	13-09-2025	27-10-2025
49	Venus	enters	Leo	15-09-2025	09-10-2025
50	Mercury	enters	Virgo	15-09-2025	03-10-2025
51	Sun	enters	Virgo	17-09-2025	17-10-2025
52	Mercury	enters	Libra	03-10-2025	24-10-2025
53	Venus	enters	Virgo	09-10-2025	02-11-2025
54	Sun	enters	Libra	17-10-2025	16-11-2025
55	Jupiter	enters	Cancer	18-10-2025	05-12-2025
56	Mercury	enters	Scorpio	24-10-2025	23-11-2025
57	Mars	enters	Scorpio	27-10-2025	07-12-2025

58	Venus	enters	Libra	02-11-2025	26-11-2025
59	Mercury	Retrograde i n	Scorpio	10-11-2025	
60	Jupiter	Retrograde i n	Cancer	11-11-2025	11-03-2026
61	Sun	enters	Scorpio	16-11-2025	16-12-2025
62	Mercury	enters	Libra	23-11-2025	06-12-2025
63	Venus	enters	Scorpio	26-11-2025	20-12-2025
64	Saturn	Direct in	Pisces	28-11-2025	27-07-2026
65	Mercury	Direct in	Libra	29-11-2025	
66	Jupiter	enters	Gemini	05-12-2025	02-06-2026
67	Mercury	enters	Scorpio	06-12-2025	29-12-2025
68	Mars	enters	Sagittarius	07-12-2025	16-01-2026
69	Sun	enters	Sagittarius	16-12-2025	14-01-2026
70	Venus	enters	Sagittarius	20-12-2025	13-01-2026
71	Mercury	enters	Sagittarius	29-12-2025	17-01-2026

Retrograde Details

Planet	Event	Sign	Data Entry	Date Exit
Jupiter	Direct in	Taurus	04/02/2025	11/11/2025
Jupiter	Retrograde in	Cancer	11/11/2025	11/03/2026
Mars	Direct in	Gemini	24/02/2025	
Mercury	Retrograde in	Pisces	15/03/2025	07/04/2025
Mercury	Direct in	Pisces	07/04/2025	18/07/2025
Mercury	Retrograde in	Cancer	18/07/2025	11/08/2025
Mercury	Direct in	Cancer	11/08/2025	10/11/2025
Mercury	Retrograde in	Scorpio	10/11/2025	29/11/2025
Mercury	Direct in	Libra	29/11/2025	
Saturn	Retrograde in	Pisces	13/07/2025	28/11/2025
Saturn	Direct in	Pisces	28/11/2025	27/07/2026
Venus	Retrograde in	Pisces	02/03/2025	13/04/2025
Venus	Direct in	Pisces	13/04/2025	

Lunar Eclipse - 13–14 Mar 2025 and 07 -08 Sep 2025. Solar Eclipse - 29 Mar 2025 and 21 Sep 2025

Gautam Institute of Vedic Astrology

Gautam Institute of Vedic Astrology (GIVA) has been established to enhance awareness of Vedic Astrology to those who have some interest in the subject. The purpose is to disseminate the knowledge and share it with the purpose of research and advancement of the subject. It is open to all who want to share their knowledge and those who want to learn through online classes, discussions, videos, and interactions. *Astrogiva.com, @gautamdkastrologer at YouTube, email: astrogautamdk@gmail.com*

About the Authors

Dr Gautam DK, an engineer with, an MBA, MSc and Doctorate Degree in management, is from a family of Hindu Brahmins who have been engaged in astrology for centuries. Dr Gautam attended various courses as Jyotish Ratnakar, Jyotish Parveen, Jyotish Bhaskar, Jyotish Vibhushan, Jyotish Rishi, Nadi astrology, Palmistry, Vastu and Reiki Master. Now he is teaching Vedic astrology through his YouTube channel "Gautam DK Astrology" and website astrogiva.com and is involved in research on the subject. He has written more than 30 Books on the astrology. Email: astrogautamdk@gmail.com

----

Sh Naresh Gautam is the co-founder and the Chairman of GIVA. After his corporate career, he devoted himself to the field of astrology. He has been awarded the degree of Jyotish Ratan, Jyotish Bhushan, and Jyotish Prabhakar. He has been practicing astrology since the year 2000 and has a wide follower base all over the world. Due to his worldly experience, he provides very practical remedies for all the problems of life, which are not bound by fixed Karmas. Email: nareshgautam2005@gmail.com

Printed in Great Britain
by Amazon

54096258R00079